DYING WITH GRACE

A Conscious Commitment to the Dying Process

Fran A. Repka

To Mary Steven
A true woman
of the Gospel and
Sister in Mercy,
Fondly,
Fran, RSM

authorHOUSE®

AuthorHouse™
1663 Liberty Drive
Bloomington, IN 47403
www.authorhouse.com
Phone: 1-800-839-8640

First published by AuthorHouse 7/20/2011

ISBN: 978-1-4634-2667-5 (ebk)
ISBN: 978-1-4634-2666-8 (sc)

Library of Congress Control Number: 2011910757

Printed in the United States of America

Any people depicted in stock imagery provided by Thinkstock are models, and such images are being used for illustrative purposes only.
Certain stock imagery © Thinkstock.

This book is printed on acid-free paper.

TABLE OF CONTENTS

Dedicated

To my parents, Helen and Frank
who taught me love and gave me wings---

to my siblings: Helenann (in spirit), Lil, Frank
Marie, Annarose, Joe, and Pat,
with whom I have enjoyed and continue to enjoy
sharing life and laughter,

and to persons and families
who do the best we can
to meet the dying process with
faith and grace.

II

We know someone by their story---what he said, what he did, how he lived, and how he died. This book is a simple story of an ordinary person who not only had an extraordinary capacity for life, but an extraordinary capacity to die wide awake and with grace. Frank never had cancer. He never had heart, kidney or lung problems. Fact is, he was rarely ill, enjoying good health throughout his long life. Occasionally, he would remark that he thought he'd live to be one-hundred years old. He might have reached that number had other unforeseen circumstances not intervened.

To Frank's surprise, death came to his door like a thief in the night. Resistance and depression would have been understandable, but Frank, alert in mind and spirit, became curious about the experience of dying, supported and sustained by the love of God and the love of family. The dying process became a continuation of life; death, a necessary part of life. Frank leaned into the dying process as he lived—listening, sharing, laughing, singing, meditating, praying, forgiving, and above all, loving. Frank never lost consciousness.

In actuality, Frank, caregiver par excellence, passed away just three and a half weeks after his wife of almost sixty-eight years. He was ninety-two and a half. His last days were truly a witness to the holy and a lesson in letting go. Were these last nine days a novena of joy, or suffering? The reader will have to decide. One thing is certain: throughout the entire process of dying, Frank was the epitome of integrity. By example he taught his children, grandchildren, great grandchildren, friends, and extended family not only how to live well, but also how to die well.

DIE BEFORE YOU DIE

Ironic, but one of the most intimate
acts of our body is death.

So beautiful appeared my death—knowing who then
I would kiss, I died a thousand times before I died.

"Die before you die," said the Prophet Muhammad.

Have wings that feared ever touched the Sun?

I was born when all I once feared—I could love.

-Rabia

INTRODUCTION

DEATH AND OUR CULTURAL CONTEXT

*"We gain strength, and courage
and confidence by each experience
in which we really stop to look fear in the face."*
-Eleanor Roosevelt

The thought of death evokes terror in many of us. Psychologists tell us that terror tends to be intensified by cultures that market fear. Notice the frequency whereby our societal institutions—economics, government, politics, and even our churches—focus on fear, highlight mistakes, assign fault, and threaten wrong-doers with physical and/or psychological punishment. Images of devastation, violence, family tragedies, threats of terrorism, and orange alerts, fill our newscasts. In addition, note the popularity of television's NCIS, Cold Case Files, Law and Order, CSI (Crime Scene Investigation): Miami, CSI: NY, CSI: Crime Unit, FBI Files, Cops, the Mentalist---all solving one death, murder and/or sexual crime after the next. Video games all too often focus on violence. Cartoons the same. Research informs us that television and film generally succeed by portraying sex and violence; and best if in an atmosphere of fear. Why is this so? Perhaps the fear portrayed in the media is one way of manipulating our human fear of death. Fear of death is not uncommon, and indeed has spurred multiple research projects. In summary, we fear not only for our lives, but we fear death as well.

Would our living and dying be different if films, videos, and TV programming for children, adolescents, and adults primarily focused on how to build, maintain, and sustain loving relationships? What shifts might happen if popular media focused more on the good people do versus the scandals, crime, and/or mistakes they make? What kind of psychological and spiritual impact does *fear* have on the way we live, the way we die, or the choices we make? Frank, whose story of dying is the center of this book, often contemplated these questions in life, and left a legacy of questions for all of us.

Dying well...

The idea of "dying well" is foreign to many people, perhaps because it is difficult to accept death as a normal physiological and spiritual process. For example, faced with the threat of death due to cancer, clients like Peter (not his real name) become overwhelmed and sometimes engage in thoughts of euthanasia, and/or assisted suicide. Others, like Mary, join the Hemlock Society, out of fear of abandonment, or fear of a traumatic or terribly lonely death. Still others like George live with the fear that they will be a "problem" to loved ones; while others fear pain, suffering, and loss, including financial loss. Some are led to suicide. Though our Churches tell us that death is a normal part of life, in general there remains somewhat of a taboo around freely talking about death, and what it means to die well.

In a true spirit of compassion, hospital personnel talk of "moving slowly" when the elderly are about to pass away so as to spare them the overwhelming inundation of tubes, lines, CPR, added meds and other potentially traumatic activities the patient may have to endure when perhaps all the patient needs is peace, and a loving hand and heart to assist his or her final journey. Hospice networks have provided an important service in helping people acquire more positive attitudes towards the process of letting go of loved ones, and involving families in the process of death and dying.

Purpose of this Text

In summary, for some people death can feel utterly frightening, mechanical and cold, while for others death is experienced as natural to the human being and deeply spiritual. What makes the difference? Perhaps one man's story of dying can a) offer some insight as to how one might navigate the dying process, b) shed some light on what it means to die as one lives, and c) invite the reader to contemplate how the dying experience can be transformative for both family and friends as well as for the one who is passing.

Frank had the most profound death I have ever witnessed as a nurse and as a psychologist. There was no terror. No fear. No naïveté. Rather, there was curiosity, some anxiety, trust, and release. In reality it was greening refreshment for all involved, a pilgrimage of great depth. Each person has his unique way of letting go of life and can teach us something. Frank taught us that dying is truly an "act of love." It is a rare privilege to walk with someone whose passing is more beautiful than one could ever ask or imagine.

This book is meant to be informative and to call individuals and/ or parish groups to reflection. After reading the first Chapter, one need not read the remaining Chapters in sequence, although the chronology may make the text more useful. Reflection questions are provided at the end of each Chapter. Quotations from poets, scripture, philosophers, and cosmologists are inserted for reflection. As a beginning, let me tell you about Frank.

"The just grow tall
like palm trees,
majestic like the cedars
of Lebanon.
They are planted
in the temple courts
and
flourish in God's house,
green and heavy with fruit
even in old age."

Psalm 92

–1–

FRANK'S LIFE: A BRIEF OVERVIEW

"Your inner purpose is to awaken.
It is as simple as that. You share that purpose
with every other person on the planet--because
it is the purpose of humanity."
Eckhart Tolle, "A New Earth"

Who was Frank? What was his social and spiritual vision, his experience of God and the world? What life experiences supported his great capacity to die well? Frank would have said that he was far from perfect; and that faith carried him through any suffering. In the end, however, I believe it was not what Frank did that was extraordinary, nor even what he believed, but the fact that there was absolutely no distinction between what he believed, what he did, and the manner in which he lived.

Early History

Frank was born of immigrant parents, who in the early 1900s, traveled to North America from Czechoslovakia. The family moved to the United States to pursue a better life for their children. Two of Frank's older siblings were born in Czechoslovakia. Frank was born in the United States on Christmas Day, 1915, just after his parents had attended midnight Mass at their local parish. There was always something

1

special about Frank's being born on Christmas Day immediately after Christmas liturgy. Not that anyone made anything of it, but it seemed that people intuited that this had to be one special human being. Frank was not tall, but carried an inner strength that made him seem tall. He was not financially rich, yet others were fed by the richness of his integrity. He was not formally educated beyond high school, but had a brilliant mind, and was a life-long learner.

From childhood Frank had a keen interest in national and world events. Around the time of Frank's birth, America was under the leadership of its twenty-eighth President Woodrow Wilson who won the Nobel Peace Prize for his efforts to form the League of Nations. Other happenings around this time: World War I (1914-1918) had started; Woodrow Wilson issued his Fourteen Points; Benedict the XV was Pope; NACA, the predecessor of NASA, was founded; the theory of relativity was formulated and published by Albert Einstein; Irving Berlin and Harry Smith premiered their musical in New York City; electrified commuter rail service began; and the first Black College opened in Louisiana. On the downside, the U.S. House of Representatives rejected a proposal to give women the right to vote, and Galveston was devastated by a hurricane.

Frank grew up in a traditional Czech home. He loved his heritage, but soon discovered he had to suppress it. Though he was surrounded with the best of Czech culture—its spiritual strength, its lively music and dance, beautiful poetry, and family customs, not all non-immigrants saw the culture in so positive a way. Frank experienced prejudice. The Czech language only was spoken in the home, and Frank had a hard time understanding English in first grade, needing assistance with his lessons.

When Frank began to write his memoirs at the age of ninety-one-- at the insistence of his children-- he wrote the following about this period in his early life:

> "When we started school, many of the kids were mean
> to us (Frank and his siblings) because they knew that
> Mom and Dad could not speak English clearly. So they
> called us 'honkeys', 'rednecks', etc. However from the
> fifth grade on that subsided when I surprised them in

class. Not to brag that I was a good student, but I was now at the top of the class. In fact one day Dad went to (town) to the harness shop. This shop was owned by Wilson Weis's Dad who also owned the town shoe store and the Pontiac dealership. So when Mr. Weis talked to Dad, he said: 'Hey Joe, that kid of yours is pretty good. He's been helping my kid with his studies.' That practically wiped out all the prejudice..."

The story is told that Frank's high school friends, who had the opportunity for further study, would knock on his door for assistance with their homework, particularly in math. Frank helped them in exchange for borrowing their school books. All benefited from these encounters.

In his youth, Frank was a member of the Sokol (competitive European Gymnastics Team) and enjoyed it immensely. However, by the time he reached mid-life, Frank thought there was an excess of money and time put into sports at the expense of quality education. Frank highly valued education and would get disgusted with the fact that we pay our teachers so little and our sports figures in the millions.

ℬ

"Your entire life journey consists of the step you are taking at this moment. There is always only this step, and so you give it your fullest attention."
-Eckhart Tolle
"A New Earth"

ℬ

Adulthood

When Frank could not live his dream to be a physician because he was needed on the farm and his family could not afford higher education, Frank went after another equally important dream. He wanted to have his own soil-tested, natural-based, ecological farm (healthy soil, no pesticides, no synthetic fertilizers,) and he wanted a large family. He succeeded in both. With strength of purpose, he obtained a job at Detroit's General Motors until he had the financial means to rent and eventually purchase a farm. Frank was bright, highly motivated, and made frequent and consistent use of the library, educating himself on a variety of subjects, including economics, law, and soil conservation.

Frank was a great respecter of ethnic cultures, no matter what the variety. He believed that unless we understood and cultivated what each of us had inherited, we could not really find our place in the world and come to know deep in our hearts what the world needed from us. At age twenty-four, once Frank felt solid in his vocation as an organic farmer, he married a beautiful woman, Helen, who also happened to have a Czech background. Well into his nineties, Frank enjoyed remembering and sharing their first date: their intimate conversation, and the blue dress his "sweetheart" wore as, touched by the magic of love, they strolled through an orchard of apple trees in bloom. Together Helen and Frank parented eight children, a challenge they said they enjoyed. Both were involved in school and church activities. All their children married, except for one who chose to become a Catholic nun. At the time of their deaths, Helen and Frank had twenty-six grandchildren, one a marine who served two rotations in the Iraqi war, and thirty-four great grandchildren.

ഇന്ദ്ര

"May you be drawn deeply into the Cosmic Dance of connection and relationship always with God leading and experience the cosmic fire of compassion and Love."
-Author Unknown

ഇന്ദ്ര

The life of a farmer was not easy. The hard, gritty work never seemed to end; but the redeeming factor was that Helen and Frank loved nature, worked as a team along with hired help, completely stopped work on Sundays, and knew how to enjoy life. Sundays were reserved for attending Mass and visiting extended family in neighboring states, or receiving visitors at their home. Birthdays, baptisms, First Communions, confirmations, graduations of each of Helen and Frank's children were individually celebrated, complete with many guests, home-made dinner feasts, decorations, and gifts. Special seasonal holidays were also celebrated. (See Appendix I for an example of the Czech Christmas tradition.) Spending some summer days at nearby Wampler's Lake was a welcome treat. In addition to taking time for fun, the family prayed together on a regular basis.

What made farming doable was the fact that communities of small farmers worked together and shared resources. Particularly during the planting and harvesting of wheat, oats, soybeans, and corn, farmers in the immediate vicinity borrowed each others' equipment, assisted each other in needed repairs, and shared advice around growing things, such as seed choices or soil enhancement. The farming community appeared to be a safe, wholesome environment in which to raise a large family.

Forty years prior to his passing, Frank retired from farming to become a full-time advocate for the small family farm. He was a man ahead of his time. Frank foresaw that unless farmers across the United States worked together to set a strong base for the nation's economy and assure organic-grown foods for its people, it would not happen. The quality of the American dream would suffer. Thus, Frank went on the road for the National Farmer's Organization, an organization doing justice work for the protection of the small farmer, and assuring "organically-grown" foods to consumers, with the hope of ultimately enhancing the overall health of the country. Frank undertook a full schedule of travel while remaining involved with his children, his grandchildren and with his parish.

"For age is opportunity no less than youth itself, tho' in another dress and as the evening twilight fades away, the sky is filled with stars invisible by day."
-Longfellow

Helen and Frank were long-time parishioners (sixty-seven years) of their local Holy Trinity Parish. Frank was active in Christ Renews His Parish-programs, St. Vincent de Paul Society, Knights of Columbus, St. Anthony Society, Holy Name Society, and served as a Communion Distributer until he lost a finger on his right hand in a farming accident. Helen was a member of the Altar Rosary Society and a life member of the St. Anthony Society. She fashioned many a homemade item and baked a variety of goods for the parish. Not a single person ever refused her culinary gourmet creations. She was also a creative artist and seamstress who had a reputation for re-cycling and "creating gorgeous somethings out of nothing", as was often said of her, to be sold at Parish bazaars and festivals. Whenever Frank was complimented, he would remind the bestower of the compliment that Helen was the real star behind any of his successes. Their love for each other ran deep. Both Helen and Frank were also members of the Czech Slovak American Club and the National Alliance of Czech Catholics.

Elder Years

Aging never seemed to negatively affect Helen and Frank. They were in touch with the young in themselves; they accepted the reality of aging. In their elder years they were new and valuable in new and valuable ways. When it was time, both turned their faces toward the mellow color of autumn sunsets, and allowed the reddish-golden glow to enliven their landscape anew. They never saw aging as a liability. One never heard them say words I have heard all too often from elderly women and men: "Don't ever get old," or "Pray that you go before you get old," as if aging is a suffering that hampers the quality of life. When one would ask Frank how he was, he often said: "I'm as fit as a fiddle."

"As I explore the height and depth of life, each discovery I make about life is a discovery about God, each is a step with God, a step toward God."
-John S. Dunne
"Time and Myth"

In retirement, they took a renewed interest in their heritage. Frank taught Czech language classes, and served as an interpreter of the Czech language for the Toledo International Society. Helen made Czech dolls and pastries to be sold at the annual International Festival, proceeds given to the poor. Both Helen and Frank traveled to Czechoslovakia, the land of their roots. In 1989, in celebration of and in gratitude for their fiftieth wedding anniversary, Helen and Frank gifted their children and their children's spouses with an all-expense paid trip to Czechoslovakia. Helen and Frank spent a year planning for the trip, working out every detail, so that no one family would be inconvenienced.

"The Grace of our Lord overflowed for me."
-1 Timothy 1

The trip was unforgettable. In one of the Czech villages of the family's heritage, a Eucharistic Liturgy, formal dinner, huge anniversary cake, and dancing, made for a colorful feast enjoyed by relatives, friends, and strangers alike. Helen and Frank delighted in seeing their children experience Czech culture, meet relatives, and come to know more deeply their heritage. It was the family trip of a life time!

Like every aging person, Helen and Frank had some minor health issues. Both dealt with the aches and pains of arthritis. Both had knee replacements for broken-down joints. Frank was slowly going blind due to glaucoma and macular degeneration, but it did not make him old. For Frank, aging was a stage in life where there is still much to give, though in a different way. He seemed to intuit the Hindu notion that we are here to make space for the other. His white hair (the little he had), his wrinkles, his wisdom, sense of humor and integrity were held in trust for others as values that matter.

At age 92, just prior to his death, Frank tilled, planted, nurtured, and harvested a huge garden that also served as a place of spiritual solitude. On a regular basis, Helen and Frank continued to entertain and play cards with family and friends. When requested, Frank also continued to assist the elderly with legal contracts, and corresponded with relatives in Czechoslovakia.

The Cross

When Frank turned ninety, he was crushed with the news that his loving wife had cancer. Helen successfully endured serious surgery, leaving her with a colostomy. She refused to have chemotherapy and was supported in this decision by her family. Nevertheless, she remained active and did well for almost two years, when the cancer overtook her. Frank wanted to be Helen's primary caregiver and asked others to respect his wishes when loved ones thought it was too much for him.

"There is... such a oneness between you, that when one of you weeps, the other will taste salt."
-M. Buxbaum

"...when he suffered, he did not threaten... but entrusted himself to Christ by whose wounds he was healed..."
-1 Peter 2:23

Someone said of Frank: "Watching him care so gently and compassionately for his wife is akin to watching an angel." How many ninety-plus-year-old men do you know who would change his wife's colostomy, prepare her meals, assist with her bath, accompany her to the bathroom throughout the night, and so much more. Frank made it clear that this was his call and though he had to cut back on other activities, it was as he desired. Helen also wanted him, and sometimes him alone, at her side. Toward the end of Helen's time on earth, Frank was so attuned to her needs that he became blind to the toll that care giving was taking on his own health.

Hospice periodically assisted in the last month of Helen's care. Frank told no one that he himself was having serious abdominal pain. He was taken by his children to the emergency room the weekend before Helen's death, but was told by the physician that he just needed to rest. He was misdiagnosed with diverticulitis. Frank knew his body well and was quite sure that there was something more seriously wrong. He, however, had promised his wife Helen he would be with her when she passed away, and he was true to his promise. After Helen passed away at their home, he called all the children who were not present at the moment of her passing to come and bid their goodbyes. They did. Needless to say, it was a very sad parting, and particularly wrenching for Frank. He had a deep, abiding love for Helen.

Only after seeing Helen's body removed from their home with all of his children in attendance did Frank agree to return to the hospital to investigate the cause of his excruciating pain. Tests were questionable and unclear. Frank knew he needed a surgeon; but refused to move forward until after Helen's burial. When asked to re-consider, and perhaps delay the funeral until he felt better, he replied, "And what if I do not come out of surgery...I promised her I would be there. We will go ahead with her funeral Mass." Frank was temporarily released from the hospital long enough to attend Helen's funeral liturgy. Prior to the liturgy, while sitting in a wheel chair next to Helen's closed casket, he personally and lovingly greeted approximately three hundred mourners and participated in a wonderful send-off for Helen.

Walking with dignity, composure, and in intense pain, Frank followed Helen's casket into Holy Trinity Church. He was supported on either side by his two sons, as he refused the wheelchair. All of his children and their spouses, twenty-six grandchildren and their spouses and thirty-four great grandchildren were in attendance. Following the Eucharistic Liturgy and burial, Frank asked to go back home with his children and their spouses to share and debrief all that had happened. Helen filled his mind. He asked his daughter Rosie whether she thought it was all that Helen would have wanted, for he desired only the best for her. Rosie responded with a re-assuring "yes"! Frank followed with: "It was beautiful...just like her." For the rest of his children, there was no doubt in their minds that their mother would not have been pleased. Not long after the funeral liturgy and a dinner for all the guests held in the Parish Hall, Frank was back in the hospital fighting for his life.

Unexpected Challenge

Frank had faith that if he could just get to surgery and get pain relief, all would be well. It was not meant to be.

While Frank was in surgery, his children (all of whom came to be with their father) went to the hospital chapel to say one of Frank's favorite prayers, the rosary. They were terribly worried, and steeped in grief. They had just buried their mother.

After an extensive and very long abdominal surgery, the surgeon met the family and informed them that Frank was critically ill due to a complete severance of the small intestine by an old adhesion "as strong as a piano wire", said the doctor. Frank's body was filled with infection.

"Who is this man you call your father?" the surgeon asked Frank's children. He continued: "…his capacity to tolerate such excruciating pain seems humanly impossible; and he had to have been in pain for some time." The doctor was right. Frank did have a high tolerance for pain, especially when there were priorities such as taking care of someone he dearly loved.

Family members were allowed to visit and be with Frank in the Intensive Care Unit. The nurses and doctors could not have been more supportive. They allowed Frank's children to be with him around the clock. It was heartbreaking to witness Frank's condition. In the words of one of his children: "When we walked into his room, Dad was still under the influence of the anesthetic. He was on a respirator and his skin as white as the white-painted

"…and your very flesh shall be a great poem."
-Walt Whitman

walls surrounding him. The room was crowded with machinery. Dad had tubes coming from every orifice. It was awful." Frank's usually strong and robust body lay limp and motionless and very swollen. In the end, over sixty pounds of fluid was added to Frank's weight in an attempt to elevate his dangerously low blood pressure. Frank had never been so ill in his entire life. He was fighting sepsis (infection) throughout his body. All his organs had been affected by the severed bowel, and were in danger.

Because his body was in good condition due to regular exercise, natural-food intake (he refused to eat processed foods his entire life), and basically healthy genes, the doctors told Frank that he possibly could pull through this illness but that it would take a very long time. Frank was quiet, and took in everything. He could not speak due to the respirator, but his children were to find out later that he was listening not only to those tending him, but to his body and his spirit. From morning to night, and sometimes throughout the night, his children took turns holding his hand, trying to keep him comfortable. Due to the swelling, they were not sure Frank could feel their loving touch. Nevertheless gently holding his hand seemed to calm him. Sometimes tears would well up in his eyes. It was obvious that he was miserable, grieving the loss of Helen, and most probably praying.

"There is something holy deep inside of you that is so ardent and awake, that needs to lie down naked next to God"
-Hafiz

Frank's immune system was struggling to keep up. After eight days in ICU, Frank also unfortunately acquired MRSA (Methicillin Resistant Staphylococcus Aureus), a bacterium lurking in hospitals. The elderly are most susceptible to this hospital-acquired infection, along with the very young. For Frank's children their greatest fear had come to pass. From the very first day after surgery his children were aware that a patient in a room adjacent to Frank's room had acquired MRSA. Each day they witnessed personnel (nurses, lab technicians, cleaning staff, etc) gowning and masking themselves as they went into the patient's room, then shedding their protective gear as they left. The next room for these various personnel to enter was Frank's room. Frank's children expressed their concern to the head nurse and requested that Frank be moved to another location in ICU. The nurse told them there was nowhere to go. ICU was crowded and filled to the brim. All they could do was pray, and their prayers were left unanswered.

I know all of the above to be true, as I am Frank's daughter. From here on I will address Frank in more intimate and preferred terms as "Dad."

–2–

"TAKE ME HOME..."
DECISION TIME

"Wisdom is radiant and unfading,
she is easily discerned by those who love her,
and is found by those who seek her..."
Wisdom 6:12

The image of Dad's swollen hands remained with me day and night those first few days in Intensive Care, and drew me into deep reflection. These were hands that cradled me and my sibs as infants and held us as we learned to walk and talk. These were hands that healed our wounds—physically and emotionally---with gentleness, kindness, and care. We seldom needed to visit a doctor, for we had Dad who could heal most things with Vicks-rubs, honey, herbs, Nonut, and Mercurochrome. These were hands that taught us to dance at weddings, anniversaries, school affairs, monthly Czech dances, and community celebrations. These were hands that taught us that work could be fun. These were hands that could fix just about anything from bicycles to automobiles, or from tractors and outdoor machinery to anything needing repair inside the home. These amazing hands, now so camouflaged by fluid, that my family and I could not see knuckles or veins. We wondered how his hands and feet kept from exploding; they were so edematous. Dad was miserable. We kept holding his hand, in the hopes of providing a drop of comfort.

After the first week following surgery, the respirator tube was removed, to Dad's great relief. Though he remained in the step-down Intensive Care Unit, Dad was now appreciative of the fact that he could verbally communicate and begin to express his needs. Intravenous poles and machines that blip and bleep and monitor fluids, vital signs, and oxygen remained. He could not move.

Into your Hands...

Sometime during this second week in the Intensive Care Unit, Dad asked that all of his children come to his bedside. He said to my brother Frank: "I have something I want to say to everyone."

There was a sense of urgency in Dad's voice: "...and I want everyone here by 9:00 am."

The fact that Dad both made the request for all to be present and stated an exact time revealed that something important was on his mind. Since we children had been rotating our visits this second week so as not to tire Dad, some had already gone home and were four to six hours away. My sister Rosie made the calls. I was now the eldest as our sister Helen died of pancreatic cancer just six years earlier. Then there is Lil, an interior decorator who keeps us laughing; Frank, who taught medical doctors, is big on "good cholesterol", and loves to hunt; Marie, a behavioral specialist, fantastic baker, and joyful; Rosie, a nurse who loves doing special things for people, especially the elderly, and members of our family; Joe, a Deacon who enjoys laughter and singing; and Pat, a nurse who is quiet and sweet. All are married with children and most have grandchildren. Dad requested that his seven living children come to his bedside for a reason, but we did not know why. No one knew what to expect.

ഇരുഗ

"We are caught in an inescapable network of mutuality, tied in a single garment of destiny. Whatever affects one directly, affects all indirectly."
-Dr. Martin Luther King, Jr.

ഇരുഗ

We were all at the hospital by nine o'clock. As I entered the room I noted the morning sun pouring through the window like liquid gold. Something about sunshine inspires hope. The sun's reflections made the sea of white around Dad seem brighter than ever. Doctors and nurses in white lab coats; white walls and ceilings; sheets and pillows enfolding my father, all white! It felt surreal, but being with family members kept us in touch with the real.

We gathered around Dad's bed, greeted him with a kiss, and hugged each other. The room was quiet, except for someone trying to share light conversation from time to time. After all had arrived, Dad asked the nurses and the doctor to leave the room. Several of us, including Dad, had come to know the doctors and nurses quite well. They too seemed to sense something important was about to happen, but no one knew what it might be.

> *"Joy and sorrow are inseparable... together they come, and when one sits alone with you remember that the other is asleep upon your bed."*
> -Kahlil Gibran

Dad spoke softly and gently and with a sense of confidence that belied his weak physical condition. "My Jewels... thank you for coming. I know it was not easy for some of you to get here on such a short notice." (Dad's favorite word for his children as a group was: "my Jewels.") He continued slowly: "After listening and praying to God and talking with your mom, I have accepted my situation and made a decision. I know this will be hard for some of you, but I want to go home... (Pause)...today."

He stopped for a second or two and continued. "I've had a lot of time to think about this. I would never have had the surgery had I known things were this bad. It is time for me to go home."

We stood there paralyzed, silent and shocked; no one could get a word out for a few seconds. My eyes filled with tears. I could not speak. In an instant I intuited what this meant, as did my siblings. Dad meant he was ready to die. "Why is he giving up?"...I asked myself. Dad never gave up on anything, ever. If there was not a way to be found around a challenge, he invented one. This decision to pull all the tubes did not sound like him. To me it looked as if he was giving up. I could not bear the thought of his going home to die. He had been so strong for all of us all his life. A bastion of faith. A holder of family values. A rock of strength. A model of a loving father.

The doctors had told him earlier that given plenty of time, further treatment, and added antibiotics he could possibly recover. In the

13

background I could hear my brother Frank asking Dad whether he heard the doctors say that if he gave it lots of time he would improve. Dad responded: "My body is very ill, it cannot get better...it is time to go home...take me home."

ಐಲಿ

"Let your soul stand cool and composed before a million stars."
- Walt Whitman

ಐಲಿ

There was no doubt in our minds that Dad meant it when he said he had a talk with God. But was he really aware of the fact that if he discontinued everything at this point, it truly would be the end? If we met his request, would we have to take him out of the hospital against medical advice? As we stood around his bed each having our own thoughts and fears, Dad, with great patience, continued the conversation by responding to any and all of our questions and concerns.

The Challenge of Acceptance

"Take me home..." rang in my ears. All of us were attempting to absorb and accept Dad's decision. Admitting that I was initially stunned and extremely upset by Dad's decision is an understatement. However, as Dad talked on, it became more and more clear that his request to be taken home was not so much a "giving up" as it was a decision to "let go." He clearly *chose* what he wanted to do.

After Dad shared with us what he desired and why, he turned to all of us circled around his bed and said: "Now I have just one request from each and all of you..." He paused, (his pauses always called one to reflection)"...and that is that you respect my wishes." When he finished, he asked Dr. Smith (not his real name) to come into the room.

Dad spoke for himself and repeated his request to Dr. Smith, ending with, "And so...I would like to go home...today." Dr. Smith in turn explained what going home would mean in great detail: that Dad had lost his swallowing reflex and would not be able to eat or drink, that the IVs would have to be discontinued, that infection was present and

ಐಲಿ

"We need one another in the hour of defeat, when with encouragement we might endure, and stand again."
-George E. Odell

ಐಲಿ

14

could get worse, and that he still had a large open abdominal wound to heal. Finally Dr. Smith reiterated that with continuous heavy doses of antibiotics and medication for blood pressure, kidneys, bowel, and other further treatment Dad could possibly heal; it would just take a very long time.

Dad listened intently, understanding all that the doctor outlined. The doctor waited for Dad's response. Dad shared with Dr. Smith in the presence of his children that he was aware of all the facts and challenges. He stated that he wanted no further medical procedures, no more extraordinary interventions, and that it was time for him to let go and be taken home, letting nature take its course.

Dr. Smith reminded all of us gathered that "Frank was of sound mind, clear in thought and capable of making this decision." He also told our 92-year-old Dad how much he admired him as a man of integrity and goodness, ending with: "Frank, you are a wonderful human being. I wish I had your faith and courage." Dr. Smith respected Dad's wishes and immediately discharged him from ICU. Instead of giving up, Dad was taking charge. We knew then that the letting go must begin, on all our parts.

Upon accepting Dad's decision, our thoughts turned to concern for his care. Dad remained very ill from the surgery and subsequent infections. Could we give him the care he needed at home? We wanted him to receive the best care possible, which indeed he was receiving in the hospital intensive care unit. I looked at his body. It brought me to tears. His arms, hands, legs, feet and entire body were as swollen as was humanly possible. Someone fondly told Dad that his body "looked like the Pillsbury Dough Boy." It was not far from the truth.

As upsetting as was the news to be taken home, it was Dad's spiritual as well as physical choice. It gave him peace. We respected Dad highly and in the end completely supported his decision. We would do whatever it took and indeed found caring for him a privilege. It was now a matter of following Dad's lead. Together, we were all embarking on a road unknown and never before taken.

Some of my siblings worked with the doctors and nurses receiving instructions about his home care. With the assistance of a hospice nurse, other siblings readied Dad's home. We children, now caregivers, had quickly managed to attain a hospital bed, wound-cleaning supplies, dressing-change equipment, mouth care needs, skin care needs, Foley-drainage instructions, and a few other necessities. Within a couple of hours Dad's home was ready for his arrival.

REFLECTION:

What have been the challenging spiritual decisions in your life?

What part of Frank's story has touched you thus far? What insights might pertain to your own life?

–3–

AH HOME!
ACCEPTANCE OF WHAT IS...

"My trust is in You, O Lord;
I say you are my God."
Psalm 31:15

The August sun was high and shimmered over the 40-acre green forest in which Mom and Dad's home was nestled. An ambulance brought Dad home at 2:00 pm, two hours after hospital discharge. Tall oak trees lining the driveway created sunbeams of welcome, and held golden threads of hope for our Dad. The cloudless sky was a deep blue and as Dad was brought into his home on a gurney carried by ambulance drivers, Dad looked up at the blue sky and gave a sigh of relief that spoke *PEACE*. His dog "Prince" stood at the ready near the dog house. Prince saw his lifelong companion was home and conveyed delight with his unique, obnoxious bark. Dad smiled, but I felt sad.

The ambulance orderlies carried the stretcher towards the white-pillared entrance of the 1970's home that Mom and Dad designed and built for their retirement. The double doors opened wide as if in warm, embracing welcome. The stretcher continued through the foyer trimmed in solid oak, past a huge triple-oval mirror which reflected Dad's supine body carried like a precious artifact to a sacred site; past a plaque on the wall which reads: "Our Family…is a circle of strength and love; with every birth and every union the circle grows; every joy shared adds more love; every crisis faced together makes the circle stronger"; past a huge statue of the Infant of Prague, an endearing Czech symbol to the family; and on toward the special place prepared for him.

Ah Home!

From the gurney, the ambulance drivers gently transferred Dad to a hospice bed near large picture windows in his spacious living room originally built to accommodate our large family. From the living room he could see the green forest, hear the singing birds, and at times be visited by deer. This was the same spot where Mom passed away two weeks earlier. Dad was at the complete mercy of his children. What trust!

₭⌒

"I long for You so much I have even begun to travel where I have never been before."
-Hafiz

₭⌒

What faith! Anxiety reigned among us given Dad's unstable condition. Love saw us through. We knew we had Dad's unconditional love; and intuited that we had his full trust and gentle forgiveness for any mistakes we might make.

Before Mom died, I saw her often, but did not have the privilege of daily tending her. It, therefore, was an extra special honor to be with Dad. Mom wanted to be cared for by our gentle father, but she was not there to take care of Dad. I made a decision to close my psychologist office and stay with Dad day and night if it was alright with him. He welcomed it. There were many of us to help. My brother and sister-in-law from Montana remained. Other siblings took turns coming on a regular basis. It was obvious that Dad was happy to be home.

After Dad was settled, we assessed his situation. Dad had never been this ill in his entire ninety-plus years. He could not sit or stand. He could not eat or drink. He had a huge, gaping abdominal wound that had to be packed. We feared further infection. Dad had been on many antibiotics for such a long period that he suffered from thrush, a condition having to do with sores throughout his mouth and tongue. Dad had to be miserable, but never said so. When my gaze fell on Dad, I thought of Job in the Scriptures. With all of Job's sores, his sufferings, and his difficulties, he never lost closeness with God and loved ones. In a strange way, I felt comforted and hopeful in remembering how intimate Dad was with God and loved ones, not unlike Job.

What made the painful homecoming all worthwhile was that it seemed to lift Dad's soul and spirit. At home, Dad could relax. Nevertheless, the ambulance ride was not an easy trip. He was exhausted. Once we had him settled in his hospice bed, his first order of business was to take a nap. As long as I can remember, Dad took a siesta at mid-day. He believed this was one of the ingredients for a healthy life. Perhaps this ritual was a "left-over" from his European roots. Every day he would stop what he was doing, rest wherever he could find a quiet spot, and just "be." Sometimes he fell asleep, at other times he just closed his eyes and rested. It may have been twenty minutes, it may have been an hour, but it was his time to draw within to the center of his being, quiet himself, until his knowing body naturally awakened. He would then proceed with his day. Dad continued this routine throughout his dying process.

ഇൗരു

*"In a dark time the
eye begins to see."*
-Theodore Roethke

ഇൗരു

ഇൗരു

*"Put your whole
confidence in God.
He will never
let you down."*
-Catherine McAuley

ഇൗരു

Allowing Dad to take the lead

Truth sinks in slowly like rain into very hard earth. The rain is gentle and the hard earth yields, as did we. Dad's decision to let go was exceedingly painful for all of us. Slowly we softened to what is. When I finally accepted what was happening and what Dad wanted, I stopped wishing that things would be different. It was then that something fundamentally changed in me. I wanted to make this the best experience for all. We all did. Letting go was essential not only for Dad but also for all of us. We needed to begin to think as Dad was thinking and follow his lead. This homecoming was not only a physical one, but an emotional and spiritual one as well.

Caregivers and Call

When a loved one is dying it is natural to want to do everything one can possibly do for the person, but it was important for us caregivers to refrain from making decisions Dad could and wanted to make. Bodily, he was totally helpless and could not move; but his spirit and mental acuity were amazingly alive! Rhythm and ritual fell into place rather seamlessly in our family. Perhaps it was because my siblings and I were practiced through our supportive rhythm of care for Mom. When our mother was diagnosed with cancer two years previous to her passing, our family decided on a routine that might be helpful for both Mom and Dad. Since Dad wanted to be Mom's primary care-giver, the seven of us children set up a system of bringing Mom and Dad a home-cooked meal on a daily basis, did their heavy laundry and other household chores. Home-cooked meals were important because Mom and Dad disliked and actually rarely consumed processed foods. They viewed anything with artificial flavorings, artificial preservatives, or

ഇൗരു

*"The Beautiful One
whom I adore
has pitched his
royal tent
inside of you,
so I will
always lean my
heart as close to
your soul
as I can."*
-Hafiz

ഇൗരു

bleached flour as unhealthy, i.e., stripped of fiber and nutritious value. But this kind of healthy food preparation was no longer possible for them. Thus, on a daily basis, we started to provide their main meal, keeping it "natural." All seven of us participated with a varied-level of skill and availability. Now it was time to listen to Dad's needs.

Rhythm and Ritual

A summary of the rhythm and ritual we followed for Dad's care is outlined in Appendix II. It included a balance of silence and engagement. Spending time with loved ones was also essential. It is interesting to note that sympathy was irritating to Dad, but empathy infused with love was oxygen for his soul. In other words, Dad did not want anyone to feel sorry for him; but to *be* themselves with him and to hear him in his need and desires.

Being part of a large family can get chaotic at times. People stopping in unannounced, meals to prepare, guests to meet and greet, laundry to be done, grocery shopping, experts placing finishing touches on Dad's financial affairs and so on. Yet quite consistently *truth and peace* seemed to reign over chaos in and around Dad. Even the smallest great grandchildren seemed to be aware that something special and poignant was happening in the living room of Mom's and Dad's home. The living room came to be viewed as a holy place and people were sensitive and sometimes transformed by what was occurring.

Caregiver needs

During this time, it was important for family members who were the primary caregivers, not only to be aware of Dad's needs in his dying, but to be aware of their own needs. In this regard, family members for the most part were sensitive to each other, and checked in with each other to assure each was getting sufficient rest. Frustration, disappointment, anger at another loss, compassion, love, and hope, all embedded themselves in our deep faith. There was time to reminisce, time for forgiveness, time for grieving, and time for openness. Dad's manner of dying was inspiring all of us. None of us knew there were just nine days remaining for Dad, not even Dad.

REFLECTION:

What would you desire/wish for if you just had a few days to live?

What are the significant homecomings in your life?

–4–

UNFINISHED BUSINESS

"Use what talent you possess.
The woods would be very silent if no birds sang
except those that sang best."
Henry Van Dyke

Thomas Merton (1915-1968), a Trappist monk born the same year as our father, once said that if we want to be truly spiritual, we must first *live* our lives, address our responsibilities, and do the work to which God appointed us. Upon arriving home, Dad seemed to intuit Merton's path to the spiritual. During the last weeks of tending Mom, Dad had no time to adjust his financial affairs or harvest his garden. Perhaps he thought he would have plenty of time to put things in order after Mom died. We know for a fact that he expected to live on many years after Mom passed, but God had other plans.

Everyday Matters

After the first day of rest in his home, Dad began to take care of his affairs. Obviously, he had been thinking of all he had to do while in the hospital for he already had a plan. It was quite amazing to watch Dad outline all that was required for the resolution of his unfinished business. He commenced by lining up all the people he needed to work with to get various financial affairs in order. It was like him to be organized.

Throughout life, his drawers and closets were the most organized of anyone in our family. Oxfords, loafers, slippers all neatly lined-up underneath lower and upper racks of suits, jackets, and matching slacks. Jeans, overalls, boots for working outdoors were kept in a separate cupboard. Drawers for clothing as well as drawers in his home-office were meticulous. Growing up, I used to delight in eyeing his workbench with its many varied wrenches, hammers, and screwdrivers all in order by size. Keeping things in order was efficient, and in Dad's mind, allowed more time for creativity to flourish; and Dad was known for his ability to create anything to which he put his mind.

Appointments were set with his priest, his lawyer, his banker, an investment expert, and with the notary public. Only his banker could not come in person. Flat on his back and needing to give dictation, Dad mustered up the strength to apply himself step by step to the necessary tasks. My brother, Frank, Jr., Dad's oldest son, assisted him in taking care of absolutely every dot and tittle connected to his large, rather complicated estate. Dad was logical and steady in approaching his financial and economic business matters. The

₧₨

"May I see Your people through the prism of Your Love, O God."
Sister of Mercy
Prayer Book

₧₨

more complicated, unanticipated financial transactions created anxiety in Dad. He did his best to navigate them gracefully, taking naps and quiet moments of reflection in between meetings.

Attending to mundane activities was steadily pursued to completion in a spirit of attunement, not unlike the practice of meditation. Meetings had to be repeated with some experts, especially the lawyer. Finances and completing his will were not all he attended to in his last days on earth.

"It's time to harvest the Garlic"

Dad's garden was yet another piece of unfinished business. Though unable to see his garden, Dad never forgot about it. Mid-August is harvest time. Dad asked for reports on the status of everything in the garden, particularly the garlic, carrots, potatoes, third-round of lettuce, and a few other vegetables close to being harvested. Most of the vegetables were processed before he died. He reminded us that the potatoes would not be ready until after he was gone.

The story of Dad's garlic is worth mentioning here. Dad had the largest patch of organically-grown garlic in the entire neighborhood. Garlic held high priority in his garden. Why? Organically-grown garlic was Dad's herbal "wonder drug." He was fond of sharing the values of garlic: prevention of the common cold and flu, managing high cholesterol levels, a powerful natural antibiotic, a strong antioxidant that helps the body protect itself from free radicals, and finally a way to keep mosquitoes at bay. Whether all of these garlic attributes were true, we never knew, but Dad had studied about the physical values of garlic and we believed him. Dad was suspicious of garlic not grown organically, or not fresh. Apparently the organic garlic he grew had higher sulphur levels; thus was believed to be more beneficial for health. Every day he ate a clove of garlic. He never had high cholesterol. He rarely had the common cold or flu. He believed garlic's anti-oxidant properties kept his immune system healthy; and mosquitoes never bit him. Year after year he grew large amounts of garlic in enriched humus to be shared with family and friends.

"Today the vegetables would like to be cut by someone who is singing God's name."
-Hafiz

Around the third day of being home from the hospital, my brother-in-law informed Dad that the garlic was ready. Dad asked my brothers-in-law Larry and Mel and my brothers Frank and Joe whether they would harvest the garlic. They told him they would be delighted. Dad's garden yielded two large wheelbarrows full.

In Dad's garden, all was abundance. His sons and sons-in-law tied the garlic in bundles, hung the bundles on the back of Dad's storage shed to dry. At the Offertory Procession during his Mass of Christian Burial, his grandchildren carried the gifts of bread and wine to the altar along with a silver platter on which was placed a small bundle of garlic tied with a simple blue (Dad's favorite color) ribbon. After Dad's burial, the bundles from his storage shed were made available for anyone who wished to take some home. The garlic-bundles were gone in a flash!

It was essential to Dad's peace that all unfinished business be completed shortly after his arrival home from the hospital. After attending to these material matters, an inner light seemed to guide his way toward the path ahead. He had an Eagle's strength.

Fran A. Repka

REFLECTION:

If you were told you would die soon, to what unfinished business would you attend ?

What might be your concerns?

–5–

IT'S ABOUT THE MOMENT

"I have learned to allow the present moment
to be and to accept the impermanent nature of all things
and conditions; thus have I found peace."
Eckhart Tolle

Eckhart Tolle in his book *The Power of Now,* writes: "Watch any plant or animal and let it teach you acceptance of what *is,* surrender to the NOW. Let it teach you Being. Let it teach you integrity---which means to be one, to be yourself, to be real. Let it teach you how to live and how to die, and how not to make living and dying into a problem."(P.190)

A Blessing

Dad's ability to touch others in the NOW brings to mind an incident I had with him just prior to his hospitalization. Dad always bent down from the waist to tie his shoes; every day he did this for as long as I can remember. One day in his elder years, I asked him why he did not sit on a nearby chair. He responded: "Bending over like this once a day improves the circulation to the brain and keeps my mind clear." His response was accompanied by a whimsical smile that I read as: "...at least this is what I have come to believe." Just days before his surgery, and because of his pain, he could no longer bend over to tie his shoes, sitting or standing.

He said nothing about his pain, but I noted his struggle. Thus I asked if I could tie his shoes for him. He nodded affirmatively. I bent down to tie his shoes. Spontaneously, I looked up into his eyes and said out loud: "Dad, I am not worthy to tie your shoes." I looked down and continued. Tears filled my eyes as Dad gently and lovingly placed his hand on my bowed head. For me it was a blessing given freely and lovingly by a man I felt unworthy to call my father.

Dad was a "listener" of creation all his life, so paying attention to the NOW in his dying process was somewhat second nature. This pilgrimage of moving toward the unknown was no longer one day at a time, but one *moment* at a time. Whether he listened to nurses, his children, other family members, nature, or himself, all was done with focus and quiet attentiveness.

ஐ)උ

"Burning with longing-fire, wanting to sleep with my head on your doorsill, my living is composed only of this trying to be in your presence."
-Rumi

ஐ)උ

Though he lost control of his body and surroundings, Dad offered no resistance to what *is*. His new reality was that everything had to be done for him. For example, we turned him from side to side on a regular basis to prevent bedsores. This procedure was painful for him, for he still had a huge gaping abdominal wound that had to be "packed" with fresh medicinal dressings on a daily basis. Yet each time he was turned and we completed a back rub, he said "thank you" with a kindness that came from an intimate-with-God place. Trust became his friend. Such dependency on others had to be difficult for one who had been independent all his life, but one would never have known it from his kind responses to caregivers and visitors. Any "barriers of control" seemed to dissolve in the wake of letting go, which in turn was absorbed by an ocean of love surrounding him.

Another way we observed Dad's attunement to the NOW, was in his perception of everyday events as alive and immediate. Dad was a family man, and having members of the family consistently at his side, whether quietly reading, praying, playing cards in an adjacent room, laughing at each other's jokes, or watching the summer 2008 Olympics on a nearby TV, was important to him. People getting on with their lives seemed to give him peace, courage and strength for his rendezvous with death.

He disliked being left out of conversations as if he were not present. I remember this "inclusion" dynamic being important to my mother in her dying process as well.

Conscious Commitment

As in living, dying was both a conscious commitment and an adventure of the heart. Every day, Dad made small decisions and choices. In a strange way, he seemed to enjoy this new experience of letting go, particularly after he worked through most of his unfinished business. Letting go requires consciousness and paying close attention. Dad reminded me of the Desert Fathers and Mothers who were their own persons. Day and night they listened to the voice of the Eternal. The following passage from Romans 12:2 comes to mind: "Do not model yourselves on the behavior of the world around you, but let your behavior change, modeled by your new mind. This is the only way to discover the will of God and know what is good, what it is that God wants, what is the perfect thing to do."

We could not escape the spirit of *presence and waiting* inherent in Dad's final journey. Though it was emotionally painful for us to let go, witnessing how Dad attuned himself to one moment after the next with such curiosity, focus, and love...deeply touched us. He was awake and aware! It was a privilege beyond telling for us to walk this journey with him.

"The love God summoned by day sustained my praise by night, my prayer to the living God."
-Sisters of Mercy Prayer Book

Learnings

In the process of Dad's active dying, I was learning something important. I was learning to BE. As a type A personality, it has been a perennial challenge for me to slow down. My calendar bursts with commitments a year in advance, and my life runs full speed ahead. But something was beginning to change within me. On these beautiful August days with the mystery of life and death in full bloom, I actually *enjoyed* doing nothing but Be-ing with Dad and family 24/7. Little else mattered. Life went on well without my frenzy.

While at Dad's bedside, quiet, waiting and praying those last nine days, I began to look at various aspects of my own NOW. I came to grips with why I might be reluctant to set a date for transfer of leadership at our large Counseling Center. I was terrified that the Counseling Center would regress in its positive reputation in the broader community. It was during this meditative watch with Dad that passing on the baton seemed more doable. Throwing fear to the wind, I set a date for transfer of leadership. I wanted and needed to trust. Dad was teaching me *how*. I felt his "trust-full spirit" in it all, though he never said a word. It was an epiphany initiated by the Spirit.

Dad listened with his eyes, his ears, his nose, and his hands. Every cell and every pore seemed open and receptive. It was the immediacy of each unfolding experience that seemed to matter. No one knew how much time Dad had left, but given the fact that he could neither eat nor drink, we knew his time was short. So did he. Coming home from the hospital and paying attention to the Now in familiar surroundings seemed, in fact, to return him to his unique and true self. Dad's spirit of love was a source of God's compassion for the rest of us.

REFLECTION:

How difficult is it for you to stay in the NOW?

What helps you to stay in the now-moments of everyday life?

Does one experience more "AWE" when one stays in the NOW?

–6–

DIVINE ANXIETY

Let me not pray to be sheltered from
dangers but to be fearless
in facing them.
Let me not beg for the stilling of
my pain but for the heart to conquer it.
Let me not look for allies in life's
battlefield but to my own strength.
Let me not crave in anxious fear to be
saved but hope for the patience to win my freedom.
Grant me that I may not be a
coward, feeling your mercy in my
success alone; but let me find the grasp
of your hand in my failure.
Rabindranath Tagore,
"Fruit Gathering"

It was not until Dad's dying process that I thought there might be such a spiritual phenomenon as divine anxiety. In these final days, Dad did not seem anxious as one typically views anxiety. He had no pressured speech, no visible anguish, no sweats, no high blood pressure, and little to no restlessness. We children were intrigued with this reality. Once he completed his unfinished business, Dad seemed freed from any concern or worry regarding everyday things. If there was any anxiety, it seemed to be around hanging on to the freedom of taking each moment as it was given by God. Henry Ward Beecher is quoted to have said: "Every tomorrow has two handles: we can take hold by the handle of anxiety or by the handle of faith." Clearly, Dad's handle was faith.

When persons with deep faith enter the dying process, I believe anxiety takes on a divine quality. For in entering the journey, one must differentiate from the group. Dad had to go into the unknown alone, and accept the consequences and responsibilities of choice. His dying process was unique to him and unlike anyone else's process. He had to discover for himself just how to proceed and do whatever it is one has to do. In this regard, we could not help him. It was pure faith which assisted Dad to intuit what he needed to do step by step. He seemed to lean into the unknown by savoring each particular moment with God and with loved ones, let go of control, and allow the journey to slowly unfold. It is the spiritual nature of such a profound challenge that involves *divine anxiety.*

Routine Decreased Anxiety

Dad and his caregivers normalized his remaining days as much as possible, and this seemed to decrease any anxiety that might be lurking. How does one know what decreases anxiety for the dying? By deeply listening. The listening starts years earlier, not just at the time of dying. There are, as the mystics would say, "unknowable and unspeakable" values passed on to family members over a lifetime. These values are tacitly passed on, for the most part. The *silent* values passed on by Dad had to do with compassion, caring, and integrity.

Dad's focused attention to his dying process became the grounding for our listening and attending. We too experienced some anxiety, but our anxiousness was quelled by allowing Dad to be our teacher of what he desired. We trusted that what had been interiorized in him over a lifetime was passed on to us, his loved ones, who were now his caregivers. It is this *experience* that is the content for care-giving, and for the most part cannot be put

"Our interrelationship with life — at both the micro and macro levels-is a learning process of mutual interdependence."
-Diarmuid O'Murchu

into words. I can only say that we tried to attend "from within", to the "unknowable and unspeakable" which we had learned from Dad. We attempted to stay focused, often without words, to what Dad needed. Our attitudes and responses influenced Dad, as he influenced us. It was a mutual undertaking; and though critically ill, Dad was a full participant in this process.

In summary, the calmness we witnessed in Dad reflects a life-time of knowing how to manage stress. Dad knew anxiety, stress, and hardship over the years and weathered these with grace. Early in their marriage Dad almost lost our much-adored Mom with the birth of their third child. Faith pulled them through. At one time or another, three of their children were critically injured in an accident. Faith pulled them through. As happened to many farmers from time to time, crops were lost in harsh weather creating financial worries for the family. Faith and hard work pulled them through. Raising cattle for market was the primary source of income; periodically, cattle would be lost to diseases or in one instance, stolen. Faith pulled them through. Then there was the loss of Dad's parents, his wife, his daughter, brothers, and all but one sister. Faith continued to pull him through. Life was not easy, but for Dad it was full, rich, and graced, in spite of the losses and challenges. He was able to integrate set-backs and disappointments into the whole of natural life through faith and hope that all would be well.

REFLECTION:

What are you most afraid of?... Life? Death? Other?

Do you think there is such a reality as "divine anxiety"?

-7-

LOVE UNENDING

*" To say that I am made in the image of God
is to say that love is the reason for my existence, for
God is love. Love is my true identity."*
Thomas Merton: "A Book of Hours"

Deep waters of discomfort and pain never quenched Dad's love for all those around him. The second day Dad was home from the hospital was a very special day. It would have been Mom and Dad's 68th wedding anniversary. Critically ill as he was, Dad remembered with no reminder from anyone. Near his hospice bed in the living room of their home was a large hand-painted portrait of Mom and Dad's wedding. Dad reminisced about their early courtship and how fortunate he was in meeting and marrying Mom. He attributed any good fortune to *her* in life and in his dying. In his half-sleep or at nap time, one could hear him say several times: "Helen, I love you…" As death came closer later in the week, he called out to her several times. It was as if he was responding to Mom's beckoning, or perhaps she was teaching him how to move through the dying process with grace, for grace could have been her middle name. It is rather intriguing how past, present, and future tend to merge around profound moments such as death.

Meditating on memories became a path of transformation for all of us, as we recalled with laughter and tears many family experiences and events. Dad had seen and talked with every child, grandchild and great grandchild at Mom's Mass of Christian Burial two weeks earlier. Some of them returned in these final nine days, listening to every word of gratitude or advice or encouragement from Dad. Needless to say, many of us took the opportunity to give gratitude to Dad for all he is and all he gave to family, Church, and world. During these visits, Dad was passionate and listened intently. Along with visiting family and friends, there was also time for singing. So many stories come to mind regarding Dad's visits with family and friends in his last nine days. I will share a few of them.

ଓଔ

Singing with Mom's sisters

"He who sings well, prays twice."
-St. Augustine

On the fourth day of being home, the swelling in Dad's body now having somewhat receded, three of his wife's sisters (all widowed) came to visit: Rose from Ohio and Fran and Vi from Michigan. These lovely and lively elderly women range in age from 86 to 90-plus. They are all bilingual. Still grieving the

ଓଔ

loss of their dear sister, Helen, just a little over two weeks earlier, they were now losing their brother-in-law with whom they were close. With Dad, they reminisced the "good old days", asked Dad how he was doing, and laughed at their own jokes. In the course of their three-hour visit, they asked Dad if he wanted to sing. He said with a smile "…of course, and in Czech." They just happened to bring their respective copies of the Czech song book which Helen and Frank had published years earlier. Dad was not the greatest singer, but as long as I can remember Mom and he enjoyed singing Czech songs with relatives and friends. By way of content, Czech songs often have to do with nature, relationships, and harmony in community. This living-room quartet (three aunts and dad) personified the songs' meanings.

Czech music has a way of lingering in one's soul with its soft and lively rhythm. My sister Marie once said: "Czech songs have a way of making one happy or sad, depending on what space you are in." Making it up as they went along, Dad and my aunts would fall into harmony. I could hear my mother in the room. As they were singing, I recalled how Mom and Dad took great joy in teaching their children to sing and how they invited us to sing in the car whenever we went on long or short trips to visit relatives, whom we tended to visit on a regular basis. Perhaps it was their way of keeping us from getting into sibling spats, but I often had the feeling that hearing their children sing added to their enjoyment. As children we knew very little of the Czech language; we sang in English. Mom and Dad encouraged and affirmed our harmonizing with each other, even when we were off-key. Like children wanting to please, we would sing all the more. With eight children, we made quite a choir!

During the visit with Dad's sisters-in-law, my brother Frank and his wife Peg came over. My aunts requested that Peg and Frank play their accordions as accompaniment to their singing. They happily obliged. Encircling Dad's bed like a living wreath, all of us joined in and continued to sing one song after the next. Dad knew most of the songs by heart. Standing at Dad's bedside, I moistened his lips with a wet sponge between each song number.

At one point just prior to beginning a love song, Dad motioned my aunts, the main trio, to pause a moment. He then asked me to get his favorite picture of our mother, an 8X10 beautiful studio photo which sat on the desk in Dad's Study for as long as I can remember. With some assistance he held the framed photo of his dear Helen on his chest, looked at it lovingly and said to himself and all of us gathered: "This was our wedding song" and proceeded to sing the song (along with my aunts) with so much soul that I thought heaven

ၷၷ

"Happy the pure of heart: they shall see God."
-Matthew 5:8

ၷၷ

would swoop him up right then and there. Tears welled up in our eyes, but not his eyes. It was as if Helen was in the room singing with him. His countenance glowed. Dad and his sisters-in-law sang for a long time, as if there was no tomorrow.

In between their songs, one could hear the birds' singing outside the living-room windows. The sounds of singing birds and elder voices merged on that warm August afternoon. No separation. No space between Dad and the song-filled universe. Time seemed infinite or non-existent. After almost three hours, I expressed my concern that the afternoon was going on too long, and that perhaps he needed to rest. Dad responded: "I have all the time in the world to rest...and eternal rest is just around the corner."

Frank (left) as a child, with his family.

Courtship: Helen and Frank

Wedding – August 3, 1940

Helen and Frank's Children (early years)

Helen and Frank's 26 grandchildren
They also have 36 great grandchildren

Helen's sisters and their spouses

Children and their spouses at Helen and Frank's 65ᵗʰ wedding anniversary

In love to the end....married just short of 68 years.

The house Frank built in retirement, complete with elevator.

Frank's favorite toy in retirement—1948 IH tractor

Dancing

Dad loved music, including opera. Music seemed built into our family's genes. Two of my father's brother's played in a Czech band throughout their adult lives; Uncle Joe played the tuba and Uncle John played the trumpet. On my mother's side of the family, my grandfather played the accordion, and two of my mother's sisters, Aunt Vi and Aunt Annie played the piano.

ഇ)ര

"Learn what actions of yours delight Him... be wise. Cast all your votes for dancing."
·Hafiz

ഇ)ര

Along with enjoyment of music, Dad loved to dance. Had he been able to dance during the dying process, I believe he would have. In reality, I believe his spirit was dancing him. Mom and Dad were wonderful dancers, particularly the waltz and polka. When they danced, it was as if they twirled on smooth glass in happy union, barely touching the ground. They were both light on their feet. Many a time our family would dance in the living room and hallway of our home, made easy by hardwood floors. Throughout our growing-up years our family attended monthly Czech dances, complete with live band and eats and treats. Never shy at these family-oriented occasions, we would dance the night away, barely sitting down. It was highly enjoyable and gave us all a workout. Mom and Dad along with relatives from both sides of the family taught us children to dance before we could walk, as we would be dancing in their arms before our little legs could independently carry us.

ഇ)ര

"We are shaped and fashioned by what we Love."
·Goethe

ഇ)ര

"No need for words..."

Dad's only living sibling, Aunt Lil, visited him three days before he passed. She lives at a distance, so traveling was not easy. Aunt Lil is ten years younger than Dad and quite active herself. They visited long, sharing early memories of growing up on a farm, walking to school, how they worked hard and played often with cousins and neighbors. After their lengthy visit, I asked Aunt Lil if Dad had talked with her about his dying, as I wanted to make sure she knew there was little time left. She replied: "There was no need to. We both knew this was the last time we would see each other...we just talked. He is so peaceful." She paused and continued: "At a time like this there is no need for words. It was a beautiful visit." Much later, after Dad's passing, I had a visit with Aunt Lil in which she said: "You know, I have a memory of your Dad that I don't think you or your siblings know about. When we were children, your Dad was the only one of our older brothers that was still home, the others having moved on. In winter the upstairs of our house was very cold, especially in the girls' bedroom. Your Dad was never told to do this, nor did he ever say a word about it, but every night your Dad would go upstairs early to read, and he would warm up the girls' bed with his body, then as we were coming up the stairs he quietly would go into his own bed. Our beds were nice and warm as we tucked in for the night. No one ever requested this of him, and he never said a word about it. He knew we had the coldest room in the house. That's the kind heart he always had."

"You're my hero..."

On his fourth day home, Dad's grandchild Mark came to see him. Mark is a slight man, single, in his 20's, good-looking, artistically gifted, plays the guitar professionally, but is highly idealistic as he searches for his place in life. Mark called ahead for the best time to visit. He wanted to see his grandpa alone so he could talk. He approached his grandfather with a hug and said "I really miss you, Grandpa." "I miss you too," said his grandfather. Mark sometimes played his guitar for his grandparents and sang songs he had written. Today, he just wanted to talk. They visited for about an hour. I did not hear their conversation, giving them privacy; but I did hear a portion of their encounter when I went into the living room to ask Mark whether he wanted something to drink.

As I walked in, I heard Mark saying: "Grandpa, I remember how you would pick me up from school and insisted on helping me with my homework. I didn't like it much then and I was a stubborn kid, but you were patient with me. I would never have gotten as far as I am today without your help and patience with me. I'm afraid I'd have been on the street. I owe you a great debt of gratitude."

Dad was silent for a few seconds and then said: "Mark, I know life has been rough for you at times, but let me tell you something: always follow your heart and be responsible. You can't go wrong if you follow your heart…and life will be good to you." Their visit was precious.

As he was leaving, Mark bent over, hugged his grandfather and began to sob: "Grandpa, you're my hero", he said, "…and I love you." His grandfather warmly replied: "I love you too, Mark." Mark left crying. His tears were endearing. He had drawn from the well, and was left with living water.

Visiting with relatives and friends was interspersed with rest as much as possible, yet Dad welcomed anyone, anytime. It was uncanny how effectively he could rejuvenate after a visit, even if he just had a couple minutes. After spending some time with people, Dad could close his eyes and center himself in a matter of minutes. It was as if he went to rest at the bottom of the sea, steeped in emotion, immersed in prayer, allowing the rest of life to float around him. He did what he needed to do, but never disconnected. When he was ready to surface, he would open his eyes, and be ready for conversation again, swimming with whoever or whatever presented itself in the NOW moment.

> *"You are the deep innerness of all things, the last word that can never be spoken. To each of us you reveal yourself differently: to the ship as coastline, to the shore as ship."*
> -Rilke

"Do you believe in Angels?"

Dad had quite a few visitors in the last nine days, too many to record here. It was a bit of a mystery how the rhythm of visitors fell into place, interspersed with his need for quiet and prayer. His grandchild Melissa and her husband Dexter visited Dad several times. Melissa was pregnant with their first child and Dad was hoping the child would be born before he passed to the other side. Melissa and her grandpa had long talks together. Three days before he died and just before Melissa left him, Dad asked: "Melissa, do you believe in angels?" She said: "Yes, Grandpa, I believe in angels." He responded: "Well, look around; I have a whole room full of them." We were not sure whether he was really seeing angels, or referring to the several family members in the room at that time.

Humor and Laughter

Dad had a sense of humor. He knew how to laugh at real life situations, particularly at himself. He was a daily reader of the newspaper. After doing a quick scan of the headlines for the day and making note of the articles he would later read in depth, his first order was to read "the funnies" as our family called the comic pages. He especially enjoyed "Blondie", "For Better or for Worse", "Family Circle", "Beetle Bailey", and "Peanuts." Reading silently for awhile, he would all of a sudden laugh out loud at what he found amusing. He would then proceed to share the cartoon with Mom, and they would both laugh. These moments always made me smile.

When company came to visit, Dad often had a joke to tell. Some word or phrase in the conversation would bring the joke to mind. How he remembered these jokes in his dying condition I will never know. For example, one late afternoon close to his death a lovely couple from the neighborhood came to visit. The couples' home had been broken into several months earlier and they talked about the kind patrolman involved, and how on a later occasion the patrolman had stopped the wife and handed her a speeding ticket. Spontaneously, Dad threw in a piece of humor he had heard about a cop who stopped a vehicle. The cop said: "Yours until nine, but at ten (over the speed limit) you're mine." They all laughed. I wish I could remember other jokes he told at this time. He loved a good laugh. Sometimes we heard him chuckling at length in his dreaming sleep. He would end with the word "o-o-kay!", said with a lilt of lightness.

೮೦೧೩

Family as sacred

I cannot close this chapter without writing a word about *family*. Family was as important to Dad as breathing. Every day of the week made us into a family, whether eating meals together, doing homework around our large wooden dining room table, polishing shoes and cleaning house on Saturdays, Church on Sundays, working together, playing together, or praying together. But not only did our nuclear family hold primacy. The extended family and broader world "family" were also part

"God and I have become like two giant fat people living in a tiny boat; we keep bumping into each other and laughing."
-Hafiz

೮೦೧೩

45

of Dad's consciousness of community. He gave his life for family, on all levels, instilling values that mattered.

For Dad, *family* was nothing less than a sacrament. He saw *family* as a sacred reality which blossoms best when all members participate in its growth. Any particular family holds the capacity to build a society for good or for ill. Dad was keenly aware of the fact that family is our earliest experience of eating together with others, learning to be sensitive to each other, serving one another; working and playing together; sharing affection and compassion; processing misunderstandings; working through hurts, and learning to forgive and reconcile. Family laughter is my laughter, family tears are my tears. We are family not only by blood, but by shared life, joy, sorrow, setbacks, reconciliations, and celebrations.

ഇൻൻ

"God has done great things for us filled us with laughter and music."
-Psalm 126

In life, and now in death, family became a way of mutual discovery, and exploration. As Mom and Dad embraced death with grace (three and a half weeks apart), we family members had our eyes opened both to death's rich meaning, and to death's pain.

ഇൻൻ

As life was releasing its hold on Dad, Dad was getting forgetful of names, but at ninety-two years of age this was quite understandable. He remembered family phone numbers quite well, but names seemed a larger challenge, particularly his great grandchildren who were inclined to have different names from those usual for our family. For example in his last days of life, he could not remember the name of his two-month-old great grandson Carson, but he remembered that he was number thirty-two, i.e., the thirty-second great grandchild. Carson's parents, Jason and his wife Michelle, who are very fond of their grandparents, promised themselves that the number "32" would appear on Carson's sports' jersey from then on "in honor of Grandpa."

Though the cloud of death hovered over him, Dad's spirit shone like the sun. He was alive, alert, involved, and as stated earlier, filled with gratitude. Visiting with loved ones brought him much joy, a joy that helped to break the bonds of sadness. He never seemed too tired or put out with guests as they trickled in every day. When family and friends left, he seemed to meditate on the memories of those moments. In some ways walking the memory road seemed to help him to transition to the next steps on his sacred pilgrimage. Though quiet and sometimes stoic by nature, Dad always enjoyed talking with people. He was widely read, and could rather easily share around a variety of topics.

REFLECTION:

Walk through your memories, remembering places you loved, events, activities, work, and most of all significant people.

Whom would you want to visit in your last days?

Have you said all that you want to say to loved ones?

Who are some of the wise persons in your life? How do they influence you?

–8–

POWER OF PRAYER

*"Let my prayer rise like incense,
my upraised hands, like an evening sacrifice."*
Sister of Mercy Prayer Book

A lbert Einstein said the most beautiful experience we can have is the mysterious. Life is mystery. Death is mystery. Dad enjoyed probing into mystery. He recognized the miracle in the tallest tree and the tiniest bug, and their interrelationship with the Cosmos. These reflections tended to bring him to thoughts of God, and Dad could never paint a too-wonderful picture of God. "Who is God that He can create such variety from the smallest molecule of water to ever-expanding galaxies?" "How can a person look at nature and not believe in God?", he exclaimed. Yet, of all the realities of nature and the cosmos, it was the uniqueness of each creature that wowed Dad the most. "Think of it," he would say, "…every human being has just two eyes, one nose, and one mouth, yet each person is unique in all the world…billions of people going backward and forward in time…for eons. It boggles the mind!" Dad had his limitations, however. He could not address God as "She" as well as "He", though God is beyond both. He rationalized that "he" always includes "she." We tried to tease him into changing, but it did not work.

Intimacy with God

Dad's relationship with God was the bedrock that gave him courage and peace to the very end. Growing up, I have clear memories of Dad's kneeling on the linoleum floor in the kitchen every morning, elbows perched on a soft, white, vinyl-covered chair, eyes closed, and hands clasped, praying. Most probably he was speaking to God of his plans, troubles, joys, fears, and hopes for the day. He sometimes invoked the saints. Saints Cyril and Methodius were particular saints about whom Dad spoke. These Roman Saints lived and worked among the Slavic people, translating scripture and liturgy texts into the Slavonic language. Dad admired them. St. Isadore, patron of farmers and the National Rural Life Conference was also a favorite, as was St. Anthony.

As a family, we prayed often. Our parents believed in the dictum: "a family that prays together, stays together." Dad taught us to speak to God as a friend. This kind of familiarity and confidence was instilled by his family of origin and assisted him on his last journey home. As Dad was preparing to move from this earthly realm into a reality unknown, it was simply natural for him to be mindful of God's fidelity. Besides enjoying loved ones, what was important to Dad in these last days was prayer and paying attention to his inner world. He was not a theologian, but he truly believed that a person is better off by having a transcendent experience through belief that he/she is loved by God. He never understood atheism.

The right prayer...

Observing Dad in prayer taught me that there is no such thing as the "right prayer" for the dying. Each individual is unique, and the older we get the more unique we become. How can a caregiver know which prayers might be meaningful for a dying loved one? By listening and paying attention. The right prayer is the prayer most meaningful to the person. Scripture, for example, may or may not be a favorite form of prayer. Music that the person enjoys can be as much a prayer as Scripture. Laughter can be a prayer as it brings lightness and joy to the soul. Silence at such a profound time is truly "golden", and can be the fullness of prayer. We caregivers learned what might be meaningful for Dad by listening to him anew and by reflecting on his prayer life from earlier years. Following are some of the forms of prayer we noted were important to Dad.

Silence

Throughout life, Dad often prayed in silence and would sometimes share his prayer. Silence was his fount for engagement and or quiet. It was his non-geographical desert. I don't think Dad thought of silence as "not speaking" as much as listening to the One who could help him on this final journey. As caregivers, we made sure there were times of complete quiet; where hopefully in the solitude of his heart all joys and sorrows could be consumed and reborn in God. Contemplative silence (i.e., no external distractions such as radio, TV, human chatter, etc) seemed to help him keep his mind and heart anchored. It was not so much a silence of being alone as it was a silence of being with God. In addition, time for quiet afforded him the opportunity to go deep into the well of his inner world and draw from it insights and concrete guidance for the next steps.

"In the midst of movement and chaos, keep stillness inside of you."
-Deepak Chopra

Eucharistic Liturgy

Eucharist was important to Dad as well. There he found not only hidden treasures, but strength to face fears and insecurities. Eucharist was also held up as vital for the spiritual growth of his family. My siblings and I have pleasant memories of our family of ten, piling into our nineteen-fifties, wood-paneled Buick station wagon every Sunday morning to attend Eucharistic Liturgy at Holy Trinity Church. It took two pews to seat our large family. Unless someone was ill, no one missed Church. Eucharist was viewed as a community experience. After Church we would exchange greetings with many friends and neighbors. People seemed to have more time for each other in earlier years.

Church on Sunday was followed by a hearty homemade breakfast, and then we

"The Beautiful One whom I adore has pitched his royal tent inside of you, so I will always lean my heart as close to your soul as I can."
-Hafiz

visited relatives (including our Canadian relatives), or relatives/friends came to our home. This too was eucharist. We looked forward to Sundays as we delighted in playing with our cousins, and observing our aunts/uncles and my parents laughing together. Sundays were always a highlight.

Throughout his life Dad shared the bread of life (Eucharist) many times, in many places for many reasons. This mystery of Eucharist is beyond words and beyond all telling. It is core to the Catholic faith. Now bedridden in his dying process Dad could neither eat the bread nor drink the wine. When Dad's parish priest was kind enough to share Liturgy at his bedside, Dad was most grateful. Dad managed a tiny piece of host (body of Christ) and allowed it to melt in his mouth. Flat on his back, Dad was highly attentive to every prayer during the Liturgy. At the time of the Lord's Prayer, we all held hands. The circle around Dad was warm and bursting with love. Mom was there in spirit. I was conscious of our oneness as family. I was also conscious that the swelling in Dad's hands was subsiding.

"Live in awe Of God you saints: you will want for nothing."
-Psalm 34

In our Christian tradition we break bread and take the cup of wine as an experience of sharing in the life, death, and resurrection of Christ. As we shared Eucharistic Liturgy in such a holy setting, I couldn't help but think of Dad's body as bread that is broken, yet how his spirit had become spiritual food for the family gathered around him, not unlike it was with Jesus whose body was broken and became spiritual nourishment for all of humankind.

"The soul that walks where the wind of the spirit blows, turns like a wandering weather-vane toward love."
-Jessica Powers

Dad's Mantra

Though Dad made few requests upon coming home, one clear request was that whoever was present on any given evening join him in saying the Rosary: "I want to say it every day....for Mom", he said. We were faithful to his request and did not miss a night. There may have been two

52

of us present or nine of us present. It did not matter. Mom was often on Dad's mind (ours too), and he missed her terribly. He was grieving for her and working with his own dying agenda at the same time. I call the rosary Dad's mantra because it is a repetitious prayer akin to a mantra, and contributed to his sense of peace.

Spiritual experts tell us that having a mantra decreases anxiety, is helpful to the soul, and assists human beings in being AT-ONE with all that is around them. The Catholic Rosary, which Dad loved, consists of five decades of the "Hail Mary's (a prayer of praise to Mary, the mother of Jesus), interspersed with the Lord's Prayer with which Christians are familiar. To provide a focus, there are scripturally-based events from the lives of Jesus and Mary on which to reflect with each decade, or set of ten beads. In his book, <u>The Jesuit Guide to (Almost)</u>

☍☏

"It is this belief in a power larger than myself and other than myself, which allows me to venture into the unknown and even the unknowable."
-Maya Angelou

☍☏

<u>Everything</u>, the Rev. James Martin, S.J. gives a brief background to the rosary: "The origins of the Rosary lie deep in the Middle Ages: lay women and men used the Rosary as a way of praying along with the nearby monastic communities, who themselves would move through the 150 psalms during the year. (Three times around the Rosary would mean 150 Hail Marys.)" He goes on to write that when books, including Bibles, were not available to the general lay public, a string of beads provided a simple means for the faithful to "re-create their attachment to the events of the Gospel."[1] In retirement, Helen and Frank prayed the Rosary together almost every evening.

Now in the evening of his life, Dad continued to pray the rosary with his body, mind and soul, often with his eyes closed. It was immediate. It was simple. It was connection with the Eternal and maybe with his wife Helen too. As the week grew on, any kind of complex prayer only seemed to get in the way of the at-one-ness Dad experienced in the rosary. Letting go of everything at that evening moment, he completely entered his mantra. There was no trying to bring something about, as in a prayer of petition, or to try to cause something to happen. It just was. No ambition. No ego-intention. Such prayer helped Dad to approach everything with equanimity. The AT-ONE-NESS seemed to stay with him long after we finished the rosary, perhaps calming any fear that might be lurking in the darkness of the shadow of death.

The day before Dad died, my sister, Lil, and I were saying the rosary with him. Dad stopped us in the middle of a "Hail Mary" and said: "Have you paid attention lately to what the latter part of this prayer is saying? Say it slowly with me..." So the three of us together, slowly and meditatively prayed: "Holy Mary, Mother of God, pray for us sinners, now, and at the hour of our death..." Dad followed this with: "...it won't be long now", (meaning his pending death).

"Thin places..."

The Celts talk about "thin places." Jim Forest, author of *The Road to Emmaus: Pilgrimage as a Way of Life*, writes that any place can open up to being a "thin place." Forest: "Any place where God meets you becomes at that moment a thin place, while whatever brought you to that spot turns out to have been not just a journey but a pilgrimage."[2] Dad encountered many "thin places." He was a pilgrim on a journey he had never before experienced. Not necessarily a Christian in the conventional sense, Dad saw God everywhere, especially in people and in nature. Dad believed we would know the truth if we set our hearts and minds to the Infinite. Other than Eucharistic Liturgy on Sunday and Holy Days, and saying the rosary with his family, he primarily lived his faith in the practice of daily life choices. In other words he was not a daily communicant in a formal way, or necessarily an outwardly pious man, but he did commune with God as with an intimate friend who cares about everything. When Dad spoke, one got the feeling that he spoke not to attract attention to himself, but to show the way to Goodness.

"May I see your people through the prism of your Love, O God."
-Sisters of Mercy Prayer Book

Dad was often curious about why Jesus said the things that he did. Almost any Scripture passage could draw him into pondering about God and life. He especially loved the Beatitudes in the Gospel of Matthew, (Chapter five); Jesus' metaphors of nature throughout the New Testament; the Psalms, especially Psalm 23, "The Lord is my Shepherd"; and biblical passages from the Old Testament depicting a just God. Being contemplative by nature, Dad allowed the Word to create an inner space where he could listen, attend, and act where needed. The light of the Gospel was not dimmed in him.

Gratitude

Being centered in God was also reflected in his attitude of gratitude while dying. Besides "I love you", Dad's favorite words in life and in his dying were "thank you", often spoken in the Czech: "dekuji." (We responded: "prosim",i.e., you're welcome.)..Whether someone was adjusting his bed covers, shaving him, giving him a backrub, putting drops in his eyes, or tending to his visitors, he consistently expressed gratitude. Not a shallow place was gratitude's source; it came from a deep place in his heart.

ൟൠ

"There shall be eternal summer in the grateful heart."
-Celia Thaxter

ൟൠ

Acceptance

I believe that Dad's life-crises and transitions broke open into grace because he was able to accept all that is. For example, acceptance of Helen's passing (two weeks earlier) and grief beyond all telling became a form of prayer. Dad missed our Mom terribly. Even in his sleep, he would call out her name and say out loud: "I love you." This too is prayer.

Prayers of acceptance and grief were also significant for family members. Gifts of faith and love saw us through these trying times. Although we admired Dad's faith-filled journey, our own feelings of imminent loss were profound. We were still grieving our mother as we were tending our father, and now found ourselves already grieving his passing. The depth of feeling is hard to put into words. I do know that the following Psalm by Miriam Winter gave me some comfort during this time:

A PSALM ABOUT GRIEVING

I turned to the wind
who howled
and sighed the whole time I was healing.

I turned to a tree
who had lost its leaves—
she knew how I was feeling.

I turned to the rain
who was in tears,
for I too felt like crying.

I turned to the earth
who understood
what it meant to live with dying.

I turned to a blade of grass
because there were bonds
I had to sever.

I turned to the sea
who returned to me
and taught me about forever.

I turned to a mountain
who seemed secure
and I asked for strength
and endurance.

I turned to wildflowers
in a wood
and they gave me some assurance.

I turned to a friend
who sat with me
until she had to be leaving.

I turned to Shaddai
who stayed with me
and helped me through my grieving.[3]

Another important aspect of the spiritual life and close relationship with

80CB

*"All things
can be done
for one
who believes."*
-Mark 9:23

80CB

God is forgiveness and reconciliation which we will address in the next Chapter.

REFLECTION:

What are your favorite forms of prayer? Do your family members and friends know how important these are to you?

To Whom do you pray: With whom do you pray?

–9–

FORGIVENESS AND RECONCILIATION

"Have Mercy on me, God
In your goodness; in your abundant compassion,
blot out my offense."

Psalm 51:3

Everyone has faults and failings, and Dad had his share. He was not one to accept only the positive parts of self and reject the tattered, torn parts. Not knowing the nature of his sins, only God can judge, I do know that he could be impatient with perceived laziness, angry at injustices, blame himself when things went awry; and when it came to matters of principle, he could sometimes be stubborn. What saved Dad from being overly self-incriminating, however, was that he knew he was a sinner. He owned his mistakes and short comings.

As a child I recall occasionally feeling bad at Eucharistic Liturgy when Dad did not partake of the Bread and Wine with the rest of the family; yet I was aware of how much he valued the Eucharist. These were pre-Vatican years when Catholic theology supported the notion that if you felt you had sinned; you did not go up to the altar for communion until after confession. (Ironically, the rest of the family appeared not to have paid attention to this theology). Dad could not always get to confession before Communion because it was not available when he was; thus, in all humility he felt he could not take Communion. He never said a word about this decision and we never asked. We knew it was between him and his God.

Confession

…..Dad's request to see a priest for the Sacrament of Reconciliation (confession) in his final days was a continuation of a life-long pattern. Periodically, he had the desire to shed the scales of any blindness that might be present. Both prior to surgery and early on after his arrival home from the hospital, he asked for a priest specifically for the purpose of confession. It is a vulnerable experience to confess one's sins to another human being, but Dad believed in the power of God's forgiveness through the incarnational instrument of the priest. The Sacrament of Reconciliation gave him the opportunity to examine his conscience and to walk through the maze of his mistakes.

ℰℭ

*"Our greatest glory
is not in never falling
but in rising each
time we fall."*
-Confucius

ℰℭ

For Dad, imperfection was never the final truth, a forgiving God was. One who places undue stress on faults and failings loses hold of the truth. Imperfection is reality. What is important is the progressive ascertainment of truth, not the mistakes we make along the way. Confession was a humble moment of truth-telling; a gift of faith whereby forgiveness by God felt complete; it was both a necessity and a blessing. By example, Mom and Dad taught us that forgiveness and reconciliation are necessary for building family as well as building community.

ℰℭ

*"…first be
reconciled to
your brother
or sister, and
then come offer
your gift."*
-Matthew 5:24-25

ℰℭ

Go First to your Neighbor

There is a reconciliation story about Dad that I had never heard about until my brother, Frank, shared it with me shortly after Dad passed away. Many years ago, Dad purchased seed-oats for an agreed-upon amount from a local farmer several miles away. In his heart, Dad felt that he had cheated the farmer. Now many years later, he asked my brother to find the farmer who by this time had moved to a different location. Dad wanted my brother to deliver seventy-five dollars in cash; the amount he thought he had cheated the kind farmer. My brother indeed found the farmer, but for the life of him, the farmer could not remember the seed-oats transaction, let alone the amount. Obviously the farmer did not feel cheated. My brother insisted he take the money anyway. Dad felt better when this was accomplished, and felt forgiven.

Faults and Failings

Dad could be impatient, mostly with himself, particularly when farm machinery broke down during harvest time or when herds of cattle broke loose. At these times we knew to stay out of his path. Ultimately though, for Dad, patience reigned over impatience. Raising eight children was no easy task and we did our share of picking on each other and having arguments over silly things. Dad was incredibly patient with our faults and failings; and when anyone felt unjustly treated, Dad's kindness and compassion always came through.

ഏറോ

"...there will be more joy in heaven over one sinner who repents than over ninety-nine righteous persons who need repentance."
-Luke 15:7

ഏറോ

The Kingdom is within...

The image of a child is used by Jesus to highlight our transformed personalities when we take on a child's freedom from any false, mask-like front. "Truly I tell you, unless you change and become like children, you will never enter the kingdom of heaven. Whoever becomes humble like this child is the greatest in the kingdom of heaven." (Matt 18:3-4) There is no split between appearance (outside) and reality (inside). What is reflected on the outside is felt within. This gift was readily discernible in Dad and affirmed by neighbors, relatives, and friends. He was a firm believer of the dictum: "the Kingdom is within." Dad's redemption was a source of good news and truly a benefit for other.

When outside issues became adverse, Dad found blessing in the adversity if it were a consequence of following inner values. Another childhood story comes to mind. One day when Mom and Dad went out for the afternoon, two of my siblings were teasing and chasing each other through the rooms of our large home. In the course of this chase, one threw a boot which missed the target and sailed right through a large kitchen window. Since a couple of us older sibs were to be watching over our younger sisters and brothers, we too felt guilty, as if we had failed. We siblings pulled together to pick up the pieces of broken glass. Knowing we had created a costly mess, we then put our heads together and pondered what kind of loving act we could do to keep the peace with Mom and Dad upon their arrival home.

It was getting toward supper time, so we decided to feed the livestock before our parents returned. This was no small feat, and we had never accomplished this huge task without Dad, as it required transporting the *feed* quite a distance. None of us could run a tractor at the time. With all the stamina we could muster together, we did it by hand. It

ℰℭ

"Forgiveness is not an occasional act. It is a permanent attitude."
Martin Luther King, Jr.

ℰℭ

took a couple of hours, and a generous amount of endurance and stick-to-itiveness.

When Mom and Dad arrived home, Dad asked for helpers to do the livestock chores. We told him it was finished. In disbelief, he asked for details of the content and quantity of what we had fed to the livestock. Both parents registered shock, yet seemed pleased that we knew exactly what to do. We then showed them the broken window. Nothing was said but "…okay, it was an accident. We will need to get that fixed as soon as we can." It was our turn to be stunned. By our loving action, Mom and Dad knew we were sorry. Such understanding and compassion was not unusual; and this was not the first time that our failures were wrapped in the sweet dew of forgiveness.

Concerns beyond family

Reconciliation extended to concerns beyond family. Dad thought we should pray for forgiveness for the way we as citizens were treating the environment. He was an avid reader and kept up with environmental research regarding both physical threats to the earth and how one might heal the earth. Dad simply could not understand how issues over the environment divided rather than united our people. For example he thought protesting the use of dangerous preservatives in food, and protesting the pollution of our air, soil, and water could be issues that united Americans, rather than divided us. Unfortunately, environmental challenges (well documented) still fall in the latter category.

Issues of globalization intrigued Dad as well. Initially it seemed that globalization was a good thing with its technological advances brought to poorer areas of our world. In addition, steadily declining costs of communication and transportation connecting us with the needs of the world could make it possible to share resources. But the new global trajectory did not seem to be moving toward health, housing, and education for all. Rather, globalization seemed to be having a negative impact, as benefits became concentrated among a relatively small number of countries with an uneven spread of wealth, and uneven opportunities for health and education. Furthermore, there was mounting

ഇരു

"The weak can never forgive. Forgiveness is the attribute of the strong."
-Martin Luther King, Jr.

ഇരു

anxiety that the integrity of cultures was at stake. Dad would have agreed with Joan Chittister's suggestion of how to develop a healthier global consciousness: "...we must become aware of the sacred in every single element of life. We must bring beauty to birth in a poor and plastic world. We must restore the human community. We must grow in concert with God who is within. We must be healers in a harsh society."[4]

REFLECTION:

How aware am I of my own sinfulness?

To whom do I need to go and ask for forgiveness?

Whom do I need to forgive?

"… ask the animals,
and they will teach you;
the birds of the air,
and they will tell you
the plants of the earth,
and they will teach you;
and the fish of the sea
will tell you everything."

Job 12:7-9

–10–

DYING IS NATURAL

*"Earth is crammed with heaven, and every common
bush afire with God: but only he who sees
takes off his shoes..."*
Elizabeth Browning

Through tears that so frequently dampened my eyes, I slowly became aware of the fact that it is the rest of us who are away from our true home, not Dad. It is refreshing to witness a death that is both holy and natural/green. Though family members, including myself, were in awe at the way Dad spiritually and emotionally embraced his dying, it should not have been a surprise; for Dad was the same in death as he was in life--- faithful to God and nature. The early Church Fathers were known to have said that "God wrote two books: the Bible and Nature; you have to read both." Dad's inherent knowledge of what to do and how to be in this most sacred time, in spite of his immobile body, drew me to reflect on his life-long relationship with creation, which he always connected with God. God's covenant is with all living things. Everything is in relationship to something else, all the way to the unknown cosmos. Native Americans speak of this reality as "all my relations." Nothing exists in itself, not even death. I concluded that being aware of our connectedness might have something to do with what it means to die well. Dad was unwittingly inviting us to view death not as a separation but as a beginning of something new; not as the end of a journey but as a vehicle for transformation and inner growth.

Many years ago author Elizabeth Kubler-Ross wrote of death as a natural part of life; that the process of dying and letting go is written in nature's physical and spiritual DNA. The reality that death is a natural part of life took on new meaning for me as I and other family members accompanied Dad in his last days. Allow me to share some of my retrospective musings during Dad's last nine days regarding how I believe his love of nature taught him the ways of living and dying.

Nature as Friend

Throughout his life, Dad was keenly aware of earth's built-in connections as she opens herself up to the seasonal dying and rising of living things. It was as if Dad intuited that his job was simply to let go, feel the feelings, and allow earth's rhythm to have its way. It was fitting that he was passing on in late summer when the leaves on the mid-west trees were getting drier and the harvest was full. The body was going, but Dad's life and spirit were ever green, and filled the atmosphere with the essence of faith and love. He leaned into the process of his dying with grace beyond measure. That is not to say it was easy, but it was blessed.

Earth, sky, water, and wind were friends Dad knew well. Never did Dad need to be convinced of the fact that the rivers, winds, and soil are inside of us. These "nature friends" took on golden hues in his last days. Perhaps it was because he grew up in the country or perhaps it was because he was an above-average perceptive child, but from his youth Dad seemed to know more about the workings of nature, its capacities and limits than the average person. Furthermore, as a farmer, Dad had a way of accepting nature as it was, whether sunshine, rain, hailstorm, or snow. Organizing his schedule around nature's moods was simply everyday practice. In his active years as an organic farmer, he listened to radio and TV weather reports each morning and evening. In addition to these reports, he did his own weather appraisal. By assessing the color of the evening sky or the ring of light around the moon, and/or reading how the leaves on the trees were positioning themselves, Dad could predict the weather sometimes more accurately than the weatherman.

Dad could discern the purity or non-purity of water and assess the

"Adopt the pace of nature: her secret is patience."
-Ralph Waldo Emerson

quality of soil for effectively growing things. Healthy soil and good seed were important. "What goes down well, comes up well", he was known to say.

Putting nature's ways into practice in his own life and in the life of his family, Dad sowed seeds of faith and good relationships, unafraid to implement appropriate consequences for wrong behavior. If a misdeed was done, an apology and/or right action was always called for and put in motion. Creation had a true friend in him.

"O Lord... how majestic is Your name in all the earth."
-Psalm 8

Knowing nature's ways and putting them into practice seemed to help Dad in his dying process as well. As the earth slows and allows her soil to rest in silent, fallow space, Dad found the courage to slow everything down. Nature's pace became his pace. Having been very active in taking care of Mom, tending his garden, paying the bills, doing his taxes, taking care of his dog "Prince," and other daily chores which sometimes push even the elderly to a hurried pace, it was now time to slow the body and mind as nature does so well in the fall and winter of life. Earth goes deeper and deeper into its Center in winter, and Dad was going deeper and deeper into his Center in the winter of his life. Undoubtedly he did not understand all that was pulling him to Center for there were no road maps, but the *desire* was there, family was there, God was there, and all leaned into the experience together.

Of all the realities of nature, Dad had a special fondness for trees. More than once he exclaimed: "How can anyone look at a tree and not believe in God!" The forest on the east end of his farm was filled with oak, walnut, elm, ash, and maple trees and he tracked every one of them. He knew when a tree had to be felled and which trees were good for wood-burning "clean" heat. Planting trees as special gifts for generations to come was also important, for trees contribute to the health of the planet. As a child I remember Dad being concerned about Dutch elm disease. In the 1940s it seems there was an outbreak of Dutch elm disease whereby the elm population dropped rapidly. Within thirty-some years, over forty million elm trees were lost. Theoretically, an elm tree can live as long as three-hundred years. It is said that the cooling effect of one urban elm tree is equivalent to five air-conditioning units. Dad had reason to be concerned.

If I had to link Dad's spirit to any tree, however, I think it would be the oak. An oak tree spends many years forming itself, taking in the warm sun, soft rains, and sufficient nutrients for healthy growth, but never more than it needs. The oak weathers snow, rain, and ice storms; tolerates knicks and damages to the self; and grows acorns as a legacy for future generations. These qualities could be found in Dad. When Dad built a new home in the middle of their forty-acre woods and outfitted it for their future retirement years, what type of wood did he choose? He chose oak for all the woodwork and cupboards. To this day it is beautiful to behold.

"He that planteth a tree is a servant of God, he provideth a kindness for many generations, and faces that he hath not seen shall bless him."
-Henry Van Dyke

As for me, the oak tree is a strong symbol for "wisdom." Dad stood tall in integrity and was a source of wisdom for our family and neighborhood. I wrote the following poem on the first Father's Day after his death. Since it carries the theme of the oak tree, I will insert it here.

FATHER'S DAY REMEMBERED

Like a mighty Oak he stood,
    symbol of endurance and strength.
Ninety two years of solid
    integrity and wisdom.

Branches indiscriminate,
    heedful, vigilant,
Arms reaching out
    in justice and mercy for all.

Big oak shadows
    one could move in,
And feel safe
    in Love.

As time added years,
　　the oak's silence
Became eternal speech,
　　a reflection of the Divine.

On a quiet summer evening
　　he transitioned into new life;
As did the oak tree
　　into appurtenances and medicine.

Both live on…
　　transformed
on the wings of death,
　　soaring to new heights
in the bosom of the Ultimate One.

"Everyone thinks of changing the world, but no one thinks of changing himself."
-Leo Tolstoy

Nature and Identity

Nature was Dad's Great Teacher. Being in tune with nature assists us in shaping our identity and uniqueness. Not infrequently Dad spoke of his concern for some children who are neither aware of how living things grow, the care and nurturing required for growth, nor how vegetables and fruits are harvested before they find their way to the family dinner table. "Too many children think that tomatoes come from Kroger", he said "…with no idea how the tomato got there. Can they recognize a healthy tomato plant? Are they aware of how crucial are the soil, roots, minerals and other elements required in producing a healthy vegetable?"

This concern about the future of U.S. children was not just a physical one. It was a psychological and spiritual concern as well: "If we don't teach our children about the ways of nature, how can they ever know about themselves and their relationships with other people?" Dad intuitively knew that it is in the

"The deeper I descend into myself the more I find God at the heart of my being. I begin to see how the kingdom of God and cosmic love may be reconciled; the bosom of Mother Earth is in some way the bosom of God."
-Teilhard de Chardin

context of nature and nature's connections that a human being attains his or her identity. Persons learn from nature's story what abundance they are made of, and how they are connected to each other, and all of creation.

Dad believed that if a person does not know the ways of growing things, it is difficult for that person to know the potential that lies in his/ her gifts, gifts that are then shared for the sake of others. He wanted children, especially urban children, to have opportunities not only to see how things grow, but also to learn how to apply themselves in partnership with growing things, i.e., to understand what "organic" truly means. It was a delight for him to teach local children, family, and friends how to make a good compost, how to grow plants, or how to enrich humus for example; as well as how to develop the skills to identify what went amiss if a plant or tree did not fare well, and what a person might do about it. Although most of Dad's children now live in towns and cities, it was music to his ears to hear that their families had gardens. I think Dad might have believed that if we ignore the experience of nature and its ways, we stand in danger of losing our souls.

Earth as a sacred community...

As mentioned earlier, Dad was an avid reader on many topics. Not being a great fan of fiction, he enjoyed reading books that stimulated his thinking. For example, he enjoyed books on economics, law, philosophy, and spirituality. In terms of the earth, he enjoyed reading Thomas Berry's reflections on the "earth as a sacred community." Thomas Berry, was a Passionist priest, an eco-theologian, and earth scholar. He was about the same age as my father and died a year later than he. Had they known each other they would have been good friends. Along with planet earth, Thomas Berry focused on the universe and the solar system. Dad was fascinated with the findings that there are far more galaxies in our universe than there are people on our planet. Thomas Berry wrote often

"Cosmology, when it is alive and healthy in a culture, evokes in the human a deep zest for life, a zest that is satisfying and revivifying, for it provides the psychic energy necessary to begin each day with joy."
-Brian Swimme

about the need for a new mode of earth consciousness, and that the magnitude of any change is in the order of religious conversion or a new spiritual birth, not in negotiating environmental treaties, although the latter certainly helps. Dad understood this need for expanded consciousness and lived it. He was a peacemaker and took seriously his responsibilities as part of the human community. He was aware that political will was not sufficient to turn the tide of pollution, strip-mining, and deforestation. I have a strong suspicion that Dad, from his heavenly perch, is praying with us and for us to continue to work with this notion of expansion of consciousness for the sake of our planet.

Nature as Balance

Nature is a catchment of sorrows as well as of joys. Dad never lost this balance even as he was moving on to eternity. Joy, pain, and sorrow, were always with him. Dad's heart would leap at a colorful rainbow, a robust garlic patch, or a lively chipmunk. Nature was never boring. Always there was something exciting and new to be learned about the ways of creation. During their married years, we often witnessed Mom and Dad calling each other and those of us who happened to be near, to share anything unusual or beautiful in nature, i.e., any different growth or new plant or crimson sky or the rat-a-tat of a woodpecker or a glimpse of

> "The Sky is the daily bread of the eyes."
> -Ralph Waldo Emerson

their favorite Bewick swans that mate for life. One particular day there was a small group of deer frolicking in the back yard. Dad ran into the house, called everyone to look out the back windows. We stood there, all grouped at the picture window like a painting from Currier and Ives, with our eyes focused on the buck, doe, and delightful fawns as if watching live theatre. It was one of many intimate moments. In his dying days of restricted movement, there was one thing left that delighted Dad: the sound of a familiar voice of a family member, friend or neighbor. Dad said what was hardest for him in his dying was leaving everyone he loved.

Nature has a rough side as well as a calm side. In his early years Dad would be saddened by the devastation caused by hailstorms or tornadoes which were not uncommon in the Midwest where the family resided. On rare occasions, crops would be damaged or destroyed with subsequent financial loss. Dad was upset by this reality, but knew there was nothing he could do but move on and plant again. If truth be told, Dad worried more about what man was doing to nature than what nature was doing to man. For example, he was sickened by any exploitation of the earth, like the manufacturing of non-reproducing seed, and the ruin of natural animal habitats. The levels of pollution in air, land, and water also concerned him. He bristled at the many farmers using pesticides. Dad was an organic farmer and soil conservationist. Before he planted anything, he tested the soil for its needs. He rotated crops, never used chemicals and did natural harvesting. In renting out the farm after retirement, he refused to rent it to anyone who utilized chemical fertilizers or weed killers. He knew that if we continue to pollute our air, soil, and water, we threaten the quality of the physical, psychological, and spiritual health of all human beings. His bottom-line question: "Are humanity's dealings with nature sustainable?"

Dad did his share of letter-writing to congressmen regarding environmental concerns. He also spoke out for organic farmers, including personally lobbying for them in Washington, DC. On the home front Mom and Dad worked to decrease the family's carbon footprint in so many ways. Long before the term "recycling" was in vogue, our family recycled everything from dried vegetable-and- fruit seeds for next-year's planting, to washing eggshells for further use. "Eggshells are high in calcium and good for the flowerbeds and vegetable garden" Dad would tell us. Mom would place egg shells in the bottom of flower pots. We would put egg shells under glass jars on top of the ground in a circle around the garden to deter slugs, cutworms, and rabbits from attacking tomato, pepper, and broccoli plants. A compost area was a given in our family. From early on we knew that nature's abundance had something to do with compost.

ℰℚℛℒ

"Nature never betrayed the heart that loved her."
-William Wordsworth

ℰℚℛℒ

Nature as Abundance

Dad believed that the environment is God's gift to all humanity and in our use of it we have a responsibility toward everyone, including future generations. Mountains, rivers, the sky and its sun, moon, and clouds all constitute abundance and a healing, sustaining, sacred presence for all of us. In other words, we need creation for both spiritual and physical nourishment.

For Mom and Dad, nature was truly abundant, and if shared, everyone would have enough. Every spring Mom and Dad would trek out to the woods and pick mushrooms for family, friends, and relatives. Because they feared we children might accidentally pick the poisonous types of mushroom, mushroom-picking was one activity they insisted on doing together without their children. They came back from the forest with baskets full of fresh mushrooms which were diligently washed and then frozen, the quantity of which lasted an entire year, shared with family, friends, and neighbors. To this day, I wish they would have taught us how to pick "healthy" mushrooms. Black walnuts and hickory nuts were also abundant in their woods and used for baking and on cereal. Basswood tea was a favorite beverage of the family, and this too came from their woods. In addition, herbs were collected, processed, and used for cooking, baking, and for healing. The family's vegetable garden (separate from the flower gardens) was exceedingly abundant, growing a variety of herbs and vegetables sufficient to feed a large family throughout any given year, via canning and freezing processes.

&)C&

"Even a stone and more easily a flower or a bird, could show you the way back to God, to the Source, to yourself."
-Eckhart Tolle

&)C&

As a large family, we lived simply and within our means. Mom taught us domestic ways to transform the bounty of nature. She was a gourmet cook who knew how to use nature's herbs and spices like no one else. She was a creative artist: making incredible bouquets of wild and fresh flowers collected from her large flower gardens. When in bloom, fresh flowers always graced our home. An elegant woman herself, mom knew how to "beautify" anything and everything.

An excellent seamstress and appreciating quality fabric, Mom would fashion lovely dresses, jackets, and skirts for us. How she ever had the time is a mystery. We children would simply point to a dress, skirt, or blouse that we found attractive in the Sears Catalogue, and Mom would create a pattern, then the garment. We were among the best-dressed children because of her. She made use of everything. I recall my First Holy Communion dress at age seven. My white, lace-trimmed, full-skirted tiered dress, admired by many, was made from the pure-white nylon of a World-War II parachute (both my Uncle Pete and Uncle Sam served on the front lines) brought home from the war. After sixty-two years, the dress remains beautifully intact. Dad was proud of Mom and her many gifts and talents. They had a deep, close relationship that held together under any trying circumstance.

"Hold onto what is good even if it is a handful of earth."
-Hopi Prayer

It was now time for Dad to surrender his abundance. He had no other choice but to follow Sophia's (Wisdom's) lead. Faithfulness and truth were his precious companions. Throughout his final journey, Dad appreciated having someone with him in a rhythm of quiet and sharing, quiet and sharing. These virtues of solitude and connection became doorways to a different kind of abundance as Dad continued the journey to his eternal home.

Nature and Spirituality as Guide

Nature for Dad was straight out of the heart of God. Every leaf, every raindrop, every breath taken, spoke intimacy with God. As Dad was slowly passing from this world into the next, we were energized to be our best through his example of deep faith, hope, compassion, and love.

Spirituality and nature are tightly interwoven. Throughout life, Dad allowed God and nature's beauty to fill his senses. An appreciation of beauty was passed on in a myriad of ways. I can still see Dad overlooking the golden wheat fields blowing in the wind like waves of sand. His sense of contemplation moved me.

In springtime it was not unlike Dad to take his children for a walk in the woods to see

"There is need for awareness that the mountains and rivers and all living things, the sky its sun and moon and clouds all constitute a healing, sustaining sacred presence for humans which they need as much for their psychic integrity as for their physical nourishment."
-Thomas Berry

the "spring beauties." I have such special memories of this heart-felt time. Spring beauties are small blue flowers, with five delicate star-like petals. In springtime, thousands of these beautiful flowers carpeted a large area in the forest behind our home. To a child, they seemed to fill the entire world, an ocean of flowers which sparkled in the sun like blue diamonds. The vision was heavenly, stunningly beautiful; and each spring the delight was "brand new." I never knew the scientific name for "spring beauties", but that is what Dad called them and that was good.

ဆဝ
"I will tell of all your wonderful deeds."
-Psalm 9:1

ဆဝ

As is obvious by now, Dad had a deep, incarnational faith. God and earth were the solid foundation on which humanity needed to build, from growing crops to feeding the community, from intimacy with God to growth and healing in relationships with family, friends, and neighbors. As many have said before him, Dad was fond of reminding us that "what we do to the earth, we do to ourselves…and the earth and God will win out in the end." Dad *believed* that both the healing and growth of ALL creation was possible if we have a healthy human-earth relationship. In other words, our best qualities as human beings and the best qualities of our earth are brought to fruition only if there is a healthy harmony between the two and our God. Dad's spirituality enhanced the bonds with the natural world.

Nature and Dying

Dad's body was going, but he did not treat his falling-apart, pain-filled body as an enemy. Quite the contrary. Dad allowed others to tend his body when he could not. This phenomenon of total helplessness had never before happened to him. For over three weeks now (counting his two-week stay in the hospital) he was flat on his back. All had to be done for him—bathing, moving to different positions, wound care, mouth care and so on. Prior to his surgery he had already been slowly going blind, and this was a suffering for him. He had been an avid reader all his life. Now he had to have someone read to him. Four days before he died, he asked me to read an article on "alternative therapies" which rested on his desk. By this time, however, he was often in and out of dream sleep, and thus tired easily of listening to someone read. He hated losing his sight, but he was grateful that he could still see his loved ones.

75

In calm and chaos, Dad's ship kept moving toward the light, led by the moon and stars beyond. God seemed to provide sufficient light for his path to the unknown. Dad asked for Reiki treatments to help him both relax and stay centered. Reiki, a form of healing touch, is a Japanese term meaning "spiritual energy." It is a healing method reflective of the common spiritual connections that we all share. It is a method that supplies relaxation, hope and compassion, offering care not cure. Supposedly, it is the God-consciousness called *Rei* that guides the life energy called *Ki* in the practice called Reiki. For Dad this type of healing touch worked, giving him relief from pain. It also gave him clarity of mind, a raised level of consciousness, and increased energy for his dying journey.

ℰℭ

"Every blade of grass has its Angel that bends over it and whispers, 'grow, grow.'"
-The Talmud

ℰℭ

By example Dad was teaching us the story of dying gracefully as he had learned it from nature. As Dad embraced the dying process, it was as if he was spiritually and psychologically walking among the dying leaves, allowing the power of decomposition and pain to boost the subsequent formation of enriching humus. Not in words did he teach us, but by example. Being with him at his home in these last nine days after hospitalization, I often thought of the words of St. Francis of Assisi: "Preach the Gospel, and if necessary, use words."

In summary, Dad's lifestyle reinforced his relationship to the natural world and to the reality of death. His nine-day dying process (I call it his Novena of Love and Letting go) was truly rooted in the earth. It had the "feel" of the rhythm of nature. I learned that everything in nature can tell us not only the story of the Universe, but the story of our lives. Dad was teaching us the story of dying as he had learned it from nature. Dad's experience prompted the following question in me: *If I am unable to perceive the story of living and dying as revealed in creation, can I ever come to know the whole of myself? Can I ever look forward to a peaceful death?*

Eventually, Dad left the womb of all that he had known, and journeyed to a strange land where those around him had never been, and of which, for the most part, he seemed unafraid. What a wonderful teacher is nature! What a listening pupil was Dad!

REFLECTION:

What image or metaphor would you use to talk about dying and/or death?

What does Cosmology have to do with dying?

Do you find yourself resisting "dying" or "death"?

–11–

PASSION AND THE COMMON GOOD

"In every community there is work to be done.
In every nation, there are wounds to heal.
In every heart, there is the power to do it."
Marianne Williamson

Dad was as deeply involved in the risk-taking of dying as he had been in the risk-taking for humanity. Truth, justice, and peace were never elusive ideals. Indeed, his spirituality was linked to the whole of life. What did this have to do with his ability to die well? The answer lies somewhere in his great capacity to be vulnerable, passionate, and hope-filled.

The vulnerability, passion, and compassion we witnessed in these final days had deep roots planted many years earlier. In addition to his love for family, Dad was passionate about education, farming, national and international affairs, and the *common good*. Not that he was an expert in any of these areas, except farming, but Dad loved life!...and genuinely wanted others to enjoy life-giving experiences. He kept up with everything: church, (if I forgot to bring the latest issue of the National Catholic Reporter, he reminded me), politics, economics, and social issues of the day. Reading and dialogue however were not enough. *"Do something for others—to back up your words,"* he would say.

The Common Good...

The *common good* needs to be highlighted here for it deeply engaged Dad's passion. "We all need to do our part for the common good," he often said. The common good was the lens through which he made many of his decisions. The particular issues that caught his attention had to do with the environment, the economy and farmers' rights. Dad took time to write his congressmen on a regular basis. He participated in advocacy issues in both the local and national arena, and personally attended political meetings where necessary. In his native Ohio, during the 1970s and 1980s he was particularly concerned about the disappearance of family farms for future generations. He was upset with the observation that an increasing amount of acreage was being lost to mega-corporations. He also worried about the pollution of soil, and water by mega-corporations and the subsequent impact on the health of citizens.

ഓരു

"Who is fit to climb God's mountain and stand in his holy place? Whoever has integrity: not chasing shadows, not living lies."
-Psalm 24:3-4

ഓരു

Dad supported his own government, but did not like big government. He voted for President George W. Bush the first time, but it did not take him long to discern that he could not vote for him a second time. His favorite past Presidents were Franklin D. Roosevelt and Dwight D. Eisenhower. He also appreciated the peace-loving President John F. Kennedy.

On top of keeping up with local and national affairs, Dad stayed abreast of international events. He identified with the late 1900s pro-democracy activists like his favorite poet and leader of the "velvet revolution," Vaclav Havel of Czechoslovakia; or the shipyard leader, Lech Walesa of Poland; and others who stood non-violently in Russia, Yugoslavia, Tiananmen Square, and East Germany. He believed in communal efforts toward justice and peace. Following are just a very few instances of Dad's involvement in economic and justice issues.

National Farmer's Organization

For many years, Dad worked for and shared leadership in the National Farmer's Organization (NFO), which was basically a volunteer commitment. He worked untiringly to draw family farmers to work together for a better and healthier country. For the sake of this mission, he sacrificed much. In general the goal of the NFO organization was to secure a future for organic family farmers and financial solvency for our nation. He wanted to bring economy and culture together.

During the late 1960's Dad gave NFO talks throughout the country, (traveling with Mom in a large motor home so they could be together and could maintain their home-cooked meals), wrote articles for the local paper, testified on behalf of farmers in Washington, D.C. and in general poured his heart and energy into efforts for the common good. He was passionate about the cause. Following is an excerpt from a lengthy article published in the Toledo Blade regarding what

ဆာ

"Every great dream begins with a dreamer. Always remember, you have within you the strength, the patience, and the passion to reach for the stars to change the world."
-Harriet Tubman

ဆာ

he and the National Farmer's Organization were trying to accomplish. In this article Dad explains what NFO wanted to do for the country better than I could:

> "...Yes, farmers may be only three percent of the population, but they produce ALL the food. Given this, what would be necessary for a farm effort to succeed? The following requirements would have to be met for success and farmer acceptance:
>
> 1. The production would have to be organized before it left the farm;
> 2. It would have to be organized in all producing areas of the USA so processors could not use cheap production to defeat the effort;
> 3. Organizational efforts would include all the main items of farm production to a) maintain relative commodity price balance, b) to prevent production fluctuation from one commodity to another;
> 4. The producing farmers would have to be in control

81

of prices and market conditions for their commodity, preferably by a two-thirds vote;

5. There must be a mechanism to keep production in line with consumption and administered with producer approval so as not to destroy the parity price.

This farm effort, if achieved, would provide 100 percent of parity and stability of price through producer-processor contracts and would not cost the government a dime. It would force the economy to run on earned income instead of borrowed dollars, it would balance the federal budget, it would correct the balance in trade, it would stop inflation, it would stabilize the dollar, in short, it would create a true prosperity for all of America based on free private enterprise. Is there a program available through which all this can be accomplished? Yes, there is. It meets all of the above requirements, has been court-tested, is experienced, is nationwide and is Christian in concept. All of the above is embodied in the program of the National Farmer's Organization."

Dad's article ends by making a national plea to farmers to work together and take collective action for the sake of the nation. Although the program made some inroads, its success was not all that great. Overall, farmers tend to be highly independent individuals, and this frustrated Dad. Nationally, a sizeable number of dedicated farmers made sacrifices and paid dues to join NFO, but not enough to form a critical mass and achieve the NFO goals. Had the program succeeded back in the 1960s, we might have a different country today, and perhaps avoided some of the disastrous downturn in the 2008 economy. Well before his death, Dad sensed future economic disaster for our country. In 2008, just after his death what he had predicted came to pass.

"How you love justice, O God, You are always on the side of the oppressed."
Sisters of Mercy
Prayer Book
-Psalm 103

Elena's Cause

Another example of Dad's passion for Justice can be seen in the story of Elena, a stranger to Dad. Because Dad was bilingual in both speaking and writing, Dad was sometimes called on by the International Society in Toledo to serve as an interpreter of the Czech language. In the 1990s the International Society called on Dad to assist a depressed woman who had been in a nursing home for some time after her husband had passed away, and her finances depleted. Her name was Elena. Elena wanted to return to her native Czechoslovakia, but Social Services who had taken charge of her situation would not allow it on the grounds that she was not physically able (she had bed sores from the nursing home), and was not "mentally fit." Social Services thought she should be placed in a mental institution.

ℰℭ

"There is no passion to be found playing small in settling for a life that is less than the one you are capable of living."
-Nelson Mandela

ℰℭ

Dad, at the request of Elena's friend and the International Society, talked with Elena several times, and found her to be of sound mind. He reported to Social Services that the source of difficulty might be a matter of miscommunication due to Elena's difficulty with the English language. Authorities disagreed. Social Services and a psychiatrist connected with Social Services had already determined that "Elena was not mentally fit" and refused to release Elena. Dad was in a quandary as he felt that Elena was capable of making her own decisions. At his own expense, Dad had her undergo psychological testing by an independent psychologist. Test results found her to be "sane" and capable of making her own decisions. It was not enough for Social Services.

Dad, again at his own expense, engaged a lawyer. The lawyer and Dad fought mightily for Elena. They were forced to take it to court. There were four lawyers for the defense and one for the plaintiff Elena. The elderly Elena was put on the stand in a wheel chair. Proceedings ran for hours. Dad was also put on the stand, as was the independent psychologist who tested Elena. They were in court an entire day. In the end, the Judge ruled in favor of Elena, but turned over Elena's entire care to Mom and Dad (both now in their eighties) who agreed to care for Elena in their home until her bedsores healed and she could re-unite with her family in Czechoslovakia.

Elena's relatives were contacted. Approximately one month later, bedsores healed, and accompanied by Dad (at the Airline's request), Elena flew to Czechoslovakia for a touching reunion with relatives. She was happy. Elena died peacefully with loved ones two years after she returned to her native homeland. The psychologist and lawyer involved in Elena's case talk about the victory to this day. They attribute Elena's success to Dad. It was the depth of his compassion and spirituality that unselfishly moved Dad to act "on the side of the oppressed." He believed that we are all part of the same tree of life.

G.A.T.E Program

In the 1980s at 60-some years of age, Dad signed up for the G.A.T.E (Global Awareness Through Exchange) Program sponsored by the Sisters of Charity. Leaders of this program were guiding a small delegation to Czechoslovakia, which was under communism at the time. It was Dad's first trip to Czechoslovakia and he wanted to listen to the impact of communism from non-governmental as well as governmental sources. He enjoyed the trip immensely, but in the end wanted more time to share with the common people. He was able to do the latter in subsequent trips with Mom. Following are portions of a letter he wrote to Mom from Czechoslovakia on that first trip:

"We are caught in an escapable network of mutuality, tied in a single garment of destiny. Whatever affects one directly, affects all indirectly."
-Dr. Martin Luther King, Jr/

> "Darling,
>
> My flight connections in New York at Kennedy Airport went well and the entire group boarded the over-seas flight. We arrived in Frankfurt on schedule and left on schedule… John Vrana, the other man in the delegation, a Catholic priest and I went for a walk and met a stranger, an older gentleman, who showed us where some of the other churches are, some of the shops, and the post office. All shops and businesses are closed on Saturday

afternoon and Sunday except for restaurants and beer gardens....The program is interesting but leaves us with practically no time to do any shopping for gifts and see things for ourselves. The people are friendly; and we can take pictures of anything except for military installations....Hopefully this letter will reach you soon. I hear outgoing mail is delayed here quite a bit...I miss you terribly and love you. Hope everything is okay at home and please get some rest. I love you, honey." Signed:

"Your Frank."

ഇൻ

"Be faithful in small things because it is in them that your faith lies."
-Mother Theresa of Calcutta

ഇൻ

Mom and Dad went to Czechoslovakia three more times, after the Berlin Wall fell in 1989. Mom and Dad loved the arts and heritage of their parents' native land, enjoyed the physical beauty of the country, and best of all, thoroughly delighted in visiting with relatives and friends in their native tongue. As stated earlier, Dad was a great admirer of Vaclav Havel, the writer turned President who fought mightily for Czech freedom. He read everything he could about Havel's written insights into politics and humanity, and enjoyed conversing around these issues with relatives. These Czechoslovakian trips renewed Mom's and Dad's pride in their heritage.

The Little Things

In little things and in big things, Dad was honest. I pondered whether this might be one of the reasons he had such a beautiful death. One grows in vulnerability when one is consistently truthful. Dad's integrity was always like fresh air in the room. He was in general laid back; except when it came to violations of "principle" and/or justice. Then he could get angry. The energy from the anger motivated him to do justice. In practice, he was known to rarely raise his voice, but he stood firm in his conviction. He believed that justice should be a consistent ethic, i.e., in both little things and big things one should practice integrity. Dad lived that way, and took the time to make things right. Just the other day I came across an old note he had copied to me. Six years before he died we were traveling on the Ohio turnpike in separate cars, following each other to a destination. Because I was distracted and had failed to get a ticket to enter the turnpike, I was charged the full fee for going a very short distance. Dad thought this was unjust. Following is the note he wrote in his own hand to the Ohio Turnpike Commission, dated December, 2002.

> "Dear Sirs,
>
> ...On Monday, December 16th my daughter and I went to get on the Ohio Turnpike at exit 3A in separate cars. I was the lead car and since my driver's side window did not operate, I got out of the car to get my ticket and I talked to the attendant as to which exit I should take to get on I-280. It took a little time...then I got my ticket.
>
> However, my daughter got side-tracked by the delay and forgot to take her ticket. When we arrived at the I-280 exit I paid my fee (80 cents) but they insisted that my daughter pay $6.50 because she did not have her ticket. I understand this is the policy, however since we were going from west to east, which we explained to the attendant, the fee should have been calculated from the Indiana line and no way is $6.50 the fee. In all justice I think the difference should be sent to my daughter."

Dad enclosed his daughter's address. The refund was sent to her. Some people may view such behavior as inconsequential or even "silly." For Dad, it was implementing a consistent ethic of justice and integrity in all matters of life.

Advice based on the common good...

The importance of the common good often entered the advice Dad gave to his children. On a personal level, a couple years before Dad passed away, I was in discernment regarding whether to remain in a pool of potential leaders for the Sisters of Mercy after being nominated by my peers. Along with other wisdom figures, I spoke with Mom and Dad regarding my dilemma and confusion. They listened to my pros and cons at length.

Dad especially listened intently. I finished by sharing that if I said "yes" to leadership for the Sisters of Mercy, this would entail a move to another state and decrease my visits to their home. Dad looked me straight in the eye and said: "You must look deep into your conscience. The common good is involved here. Whenever the common good is at stake, you must look deep. There is much suffering in this world, and in leading the Sisters of Mercy, perhaps you could bring a new focus on how to address the suffering. You are a natural, born leader. I'm not saying you should do it, but you must look deep into your conscience. And don't factor Mom and me into the equation. We will be fine with your moving out of state. "We know you love us and we love you very much. We know you'll come to visit us whenever you can. You will be in our prayers in a special way at this time. If you say yes, I know you will have to sacrifice some things, some goals you've had for yourself. But the *common good* is at stake and must be taken seriously." Mom affirmatively nodded. At the end of the conversation, Dad again ended with: "You, Frances, must look deep into your conscience." I was filled with tears at the beauty and depth of my 91-year-old father who was as profound, faith-filled, and caring as ever. Again, he touched my confusion with clarity.

"All things can be done for the one who believes."
-Mark 9:23

In the end I decided to continue in ministry as Executive Director of Mercy Counseling Center for the poor where I had worked for many years. There were no other nun-psychologists to take the position. The common good could be served here as well. Another factor: my mother's cancer had taken a turn for the worse by the time of formal discernment for leadership. I wanted to be accessible. One thing I knew for sure, Mom and Dad would support whatever decision I made. They always had.

REFLECTION:

What would it mean to focus on the common good in your own community?

How can you build a community where the gifts and special needs of all are honored and respected?

Do you challenge your politicians and government to live up to their responsibilities?

Through your own gifts and talents, how do you imagine making our world a life-giving place for all?

–12–

AN ENCOUNTER WITH GOD
AT 4:00 A.M.

"Jesus took with him Peter, John, and James,
and went up on the mountain to pray.
And while he was praying,
The appearance of his face changed,
and his clothes became dazzling white."
-Luke 9:28-29

D ad's final journey on earth was purposeful and meaningful.
Three days before he died, Dad's swollen body was back to
normal size except for his ankles which remained edematous.
This release of pressure on his organs and overall body considerably
decreased his pain. It felt good to him. Throughout his last days, we
were aware that Dad had intense pain by reading his face and hearing
him moan whenever we moved him from side to side to prevent bed
sores. Yet he said not a word about his pain. He was a silent sufferer,
and refused pain medication because, he said "it would dull my senses."
A good back rub or Reiki treatment would sometimes relieve the pain,
but not always.

The sixth day of being at home, i.e., three days before he died, Dad
awakened at four o'clock in the morning and called my name. I quickly

went over to his bedside fearing something was wrong. His voice was rather light and enthusiastic. He spoke clearly and said:

"You know, I feel like myself again for the first time since I took ill. I don't have pain and I feel good. What do you think God is telling me?"

I said: "I don't know, Dad, what do you think God is telling you?"

"This is a new moment. I think God might be telling me to continue on here…my body feels better. What would I need to do to get stronger?" he asked.

I responded softly and clearly: "Well… Dad, you have had nothing to eat or drink for over three weeks now. A week ago you had IV fluids while in the hospital, but for the last six days, you have had no fluid intake. Your intestines have been dormant, you have no bowel sounds, and you have lost your swallowing reflex. To get stronger, you will need to first try to drink some fluid …then slowly begin to eat something." My brother Frank was also present.

Dad turned to me and said: "Go get me some water." I was anxious as I feared that Dad would aspirate, and catch pneumonia. Nevertheless at his request, I went to get a small glass of water, placed an elbow-straw in the glass and allowed Dad to slowly sip

"You will show me the path… You will fill me with the joy of your presence, the delights at your hand forever."
-Psalm 16:1

"In the morning when I began to wake, it happened again--- that feeling that You, Beloved, had stood over me all night keeping watch, that feeling that as soon as I began to stir You put your lips on my forehead and lit a Holy Lamp inside my heart."
-Hafiz

the water from his supine position. It was a bit of a challenge because he could not sit up, and remained physically weak. To our surprise he could swallow by taking very tiny sips of water at a time. Three sips were all he could handle at that moment, but he was pleased he could swallow without choking.

He then said: "Now please make me some homemade chicken soup. Not plain broth. I want the vegetables too. Chop up the carrots, potatoes, celery, and onion real fine and put them in the soup."

Dad was remembering Mom's home-made recipe made with home-grown chicken. I knew I did not have her touch, but I would try to fulfill his wish: "Dad, I will be happy to cook chicken soup, but how about if we go back to sleep until 6:00, and then I will make the soup."

"That will be fine. Thank you," he said.

At 6:00 am I arose to make Dad his favorite chicken soup, exactly as he ordered. I recalled how chicken soup was his cure for colds, aches, and pains. I did it with love as well as some fear and trepidation that he could aspirate the soup into his lungs. Dad enjoyed smelling the chicken soup in process. I strained and pureed the vegetables, returned them to the soup, then approached Dad's bed with a small cup. It was difficult to get the soup to his mouth without his choking on the liquid.

"One day He did not leave after kissing me."
-Rabia

We began with one teaspoon the first half-hour, two teaspoons the second half-hour. He took them quite well. We rested in between. However, as we approached the third half-hour he began to choke and said he did not feel well. After he sipped one last teaspoon, he said: "I have my answer from God. I don't want anymore. My body just can't do it." His favorite chicken soup was served to guests. Dad went back to sleep. He was now sleeping much of the day. His body was physically shutting down and preparing to stop. Interrelatedly, his spirit seemed to hover between this realm and the next. Yes, this was a new moment, an epiphany, a close encounter with God. Peace was written on Dad's face, and his heart continued to guide him like a lantern in the night.

REFLECTION:

What were/are some of your "epiphanies", i.e., your experiences of the Holy One in the midst of your everyday world?

What do you think God was telling Frank as conveyed in this Chapter?

–13–

DAD'S LAST DAY

"I am going to prepare a place for you...
So that where I am you may be too."
John 14:2-3

There is no delaying the advent of death; and no amount of "wishing" can keep our loved ones from death. Dad had come to the edge of all he had known. The unknown now beckoned. No one knew this would be his final day for he continued to be quite alert and his memory was good. Though earth still held his body, unbeknownst to us, he was already being given wings. He continued to live in a spirit of gratitude, saying "thank you" for even the smallest ministrations. Mom was still on his mind as he spoke one "I love you" after the next to her and to all of us present. Now in his last hours, he was often in a semi-sleep state. The previous night he called out to my sister Rosie and said that he was thirsty. When she approached his bed, he said: "Oh, Helen you look so beautiful!" We concluded that he was again dreaming of our mother.

At one point on this last day, Dad exclaimed: "Where is that light coming from?" He had had his eyes closed. I replied: "Dad, I don't know, but keep going toward

ಬ⊃ಀ

"I will love the light
for it shows me the
way, yet I will endure
the darkness because
it shows me the stars."
-Og Mandin

ಬ⊃ಀ

93

the light." He smiled a smile of recognition and with assurance in his voice, coupled with a bit of lilt, exclaimed: "Yes!" Yes!" This process of dying was no naïve undertaking. It was mystery filled with wonder and hope.

As mentioned earlier, Mom and Dad's grandchild Melissa was about to deliver her first baby, and Dad was hoping the baby would arrive before he passed. On this, his last day, the phone rang early in the morning. My sister Lil answered it. She repeated the information as she was receiving it from my sister Rosie, the grandmother. I in turn relayed it in Dad's ear: "Melissa had a baby girl, six pounds, eleven ounces, twenty-one inches long, delivered at eight-something this morning. Her name is Anna Pauline." Dad smiled big at the news and remembered out loud that this was his 34th great grandchild. He was proud. His glowing countenance put me in mind of a picture I once saw depicting the Biblical Simeon's joy-filled face when he first saw the Christ child. Dad's face, like Simeon's, was aglow and filled with gratitude to God, wishing the best for the child.

ଛୠଔ

"Our days pass by like grass, our prime like a flower in bloom. A wind comes; the flower goes, empty now its place."
-Psalm 103

ଛୠଔ

Dad's mother and daughter carry the name Anna, the name given to this newest great grandchild. As for me, I was keenly aware that as one family member was entering the world, another was leaving all too quickly.

Dad slept most of the day. He seemed to need it. The hospice nurse came in to change his abdominal dressing. We were happy to see that Nadine (Mom's favorite hospice nurse) would now be Dad's regular Hospice nurse. My sister Marie and her husband Charlie came for a visit for a few hours in the afternoon. After they left, Lil and Larry and I said the Rosary around Dad's bed. Dad no longer had the energy to say it aloud, but he was conscious and could hear. After the rosary, family members present went to eat supper in the dining room, allowing Dad to sleep. After supper we played a card game. Dad loved cards and enjoyed hearing his children getting excited over card games.

Later that evening as we sat with Dad in quiet, we detected a rattle. The atropine we gave him to dry up the secretions did not seem effective this time. I did some healing touch for him, and then Lil and I gave him a back rub with the hope that the activity would move the secretions. It helped little. Dad was anxious. I was getting anxious. I feared Dad was acquiring pneumonia. I asked if he wanted us to call the hospice nurse. He shook his head "yes." I called. It took 45 minutes or so for her to arrive. By 11:00 pm she arrived. The nurse checked him, said his lower lungs were clear and that the secretions were shallow, working their way out. "No worry about pneumonia" she informed us. We were relieved. Dad seemed relieved as well, and more relaxed. As I walked the nurse to the door, I asked her if the time was close, for I sensed a different aura around Dad. She said: "Your father is still quite alert and can express his needs. I have been in this work for years; he has at least a couple more days." I took her at her word, but it wasn't true.

Dad's last breath...

My brother Frank, Jr. and his wife Peg came home from an evening function. I and my sister Lil and her husband Larry stayed up until midnight. Peg and Frank wanted to stay with Dad this night since other sibs had the privilege the two previous nights (we were taking turns so that someone would be with Dad each night). As always, I kissed Dad goodnight and said "I love you." At 1:08 my brother awakened me as well as my sister Lil and her husband Larry. Dad was just a breath away from death's embrace. He took his last breath peacefully. We called our siblings who were not present, and comforted each other.

"Into your hands, O God, I commend my Spirit."
-Psalm 31

Dad died on August 12, 2008 near the *time* of night he was born, i.e., after midnight Mass on Christmas Day, 1915. He had come full circle. He never seemed to lose consciousness, just peacefully slept away with five of his children keeping vigil. As the angels took him to paradise, we stayed with Dad, saying our goodbyes for the last time. It was a long, sacred night. Dad had emptied himself with unending love. We caregivers came to believe that death is truly an act of love.

As we stood watch with Dad throughout his final pilgrimage, it was inexhaustible sweetness. On another level, it felt as if our hearts were being ripped apart, with no hope of being patched together again. His dying was a profound experience of courage, trust, faith, and deep love, but also a painful separation and unimaginable felt loss. Our horizon was now shrouded in a silent thick mist.

After Dad died, I found myself screaming within: "Does the world have any idea what a loving couple it lost in a matter of three and a half weeks? Why do people have to die? Why can't they live forever? God, why did you ever invent such a reality as death? These were two wonderful human beings who contributed so much..." Does anyone care? Then I would hear an echo of Mom's and Dad's voice saying: "I love you" or "Thank you" and all would seem okay again.

ഉറവ

*"Wherever I go—
only Thou!
Wherever I stand—
only Thou!."*
-Hasidic Song

ഉറവ

But for awhile it wasn't okay. Loss is a cross. The world seemed to stop. I ceased writing in my journal. Together with my sibs, we once again went through the motions of preparing for a funeral liturgy and burial. It seemed only yesterday we did this for our Mom.

Three weeks after laying Dad to rest, I started to write in my journal again. A partial entry reads: "My tears continue to flow like rain that never stops. It is pouring today in Cincinnati and nature needs it. Most probably the rain is a leftover from hurricane Gustav or perhaps Fay. I miss Mom and Dad so much. Nature's tears are in solidarity with mine.

Earlier this week when I took a swim after working with our poor clients all day, I felt as if I were swimming in a pool of tears. I think of Mom and Dad all the time. What great people. What wonderful parents! What love they brought to our world! Thank you, God, for the gift. My grief is so deep ...and profoundly painful. Only Mom and Dad's love give the grief any relief."

Many pass through the process of dying with no notice of its many faces. For Mom and Dad, death was a friend. Each had climbed a mountain, laid down their load, shed their burdens. When it was time, they did not cling. Mom, beautiful, gifted, faith-filled, wife and mother *par excellance*, slowly

ഉറവ

*"This day is holy to
the Lord your God;
do not mourn or
weep. This day is holy
to our Lord; and do
not be grieved, for
the joy of the Lord
is your strength."*
-Nehemiah 8:96, 106

ഉറവ

wasted away from cancer, yet remained conscious until two days before she passed, with Dad and some of her children around her.

Dad, who had been very active, highly competent, hardworking, thinking of others on a consistent basis, and who remained conscious to the end had an astounding ability to let go and allow reality to unfold as it will. Death was the kindest friend to him that I have ever witnessed with anyone. It was almost as if the mystery of death gently enveloped any suffering, and taught Dad, step by step, how to let go. And there were numerous *letting-go's* witnessed by all of us:

Letting go of his wife of almost 68 years,
Letting go of the past (forgiveness),
Letting go of the future,
Letting go of independence,
Letting go of time,
Letting go of loved ones, especially his children, grandchildren, and great grand-children,
Letting go of his only living sister, other relatives, friends, and neighbors,
Letting go of control,
Letting go of any further concerns,
Letting go of all that for which he had worked hard,
Letting go of anything that may be unfinished,
Letting go of life as he knew it and loved it.

I believe it was Dad's intimacy with God, with Mom, and his in-touchness with nature that assisted him gracefully through the dying process. Witnessing his last days, and how much we had learned how not to be afraid, inspired the following Haiku:

On the wings of death
Does our lightness of being
Soar to new heights.

REFLECTION:

How have you experienced joy from being a transformative power for good?

What kinds of "letting go" do you need to do in order to grow in wholeness and holiness?

What gifts do you bring to the dying process?

-14-

LIVING WITH GRIEF

"In our sleep, pain which cannot forget
falls drop by drop upon the heart
until in our own despair, against our will,
comes wisdom through the awful grace of God."
Aeschylus

Grief is a personal journey. Each of us siblings had our own unique way of mourning the loss of Mom and Dad who were both embraced by death within three and a half weeks of each other. For some of my siblings, tears flowed like water, for others a kind of numbness quelled the tears. For some, a long walk to dissipate the after-shock was the choice, while others needed a quiet place to rest for long moments. Some wanted to talk about their feelings, others did not. For all of us, the world became a different, strange place with an otherworldly quality. Things seemed surreal, as if looking through a rain-soaked window. We were in disbelief that both of our parents were gone. Belief is painful. And when belief is painful, denial can cast a threatening shadow.

ॐ ঙ

"Death ends a life,
not a relationship."
-Robert Benchley

ॐ ঙ

Planning Mom and Dad's funeral liturgies and burials, (i.e. not leaving the preparation to a parish bereavement committee, which was kindly offered to us) helped us children to grieve. Working together on every aspect of the Mass of Christian burial with the deep faith we were given, seemed to move us through denial and into the bittersweet experience of acceptance.

Reminders of Mom and Dad and their spirit spontaneously arose on a regular basis, for all of us. As for me, in the middle of the city where I live, I hear morning doves that I never before heard with such frequency. Mom loved the gentle "coo" of the morning dove's song. She sings to me every time I hear the dove's morning call. In addition, I find myself decorating a room through Mom's eyes, creating cards with her touch. Continued enjoyment of my great nieces and nephews puts Mom right in the room with me.

Dad's love for trees, respect of nature, and most especially his love for truth and justice moves me still, and encourages me to continue my work for justice, peace, and integrity of creation. I prepare breakfast much like he did: steel-cut oats with milk, topped with half an apple, blueberries or strawberries, a half a banana, and almonds. I take time to read the Sunday comics, not being embarrassed to laugh out loud.

ಬಿಲ್ಲ

"The secret... for both mind and body is not to mourn the past, not to worry about the future... but to live the present moment wisely and earnestly."
-Siddartha Guatama Buddha

ಬಿಲ್ಲ

In my journey of mourning, I discovered that grief does not have an on and off switch. There were days when the pain of loss was intense. Other days were "normal." I never knew how I would feel from one day to the next. The shock didn't happen just once, it happened over and over. A month or so after they were gone, I made a silent retreat in nature. I exercised, ate well, took long nature walks, journaled my feelings, and wrote poetry. The retreat helped. Yet grief was persistent and followed me everywhere. I painted a living-room wall slowly, deliberately, and to soft music. Memories poured in. I spent time with family, friends, and my Sisters in community. I practiced mindfulness, a compassionate and accepting attitude toward my feelings and thoughts, however they arose. All of the above helped to assuage the pain of loss. It took me over a year to feel somewhat whole again.

Then the holidays arrived. Holidays were especially challenging.

There was no Mom and Dad to lead our family Christmas ritual and celebration. Halloween, at which time Mom and Dad would host a huge costume party in their decorated barn, complete with hayrides, would happen no more. Easter with its special dinner, and Easter-egg hunts first for the little ones, then the little ones wanting to hide the eggs for the adults while Mom and Dad sat on the porch thoroughly enjoying the wildness of it all, is now just a memory. Thanksgiving dinner filled with prayers of gratitude, any needed reconciliation, and love, modeled by Mom and Dad, now a thing of the past. Life goes on.

Family reunions, religious events such as Baptisms, First Communions, Confirmations, various anniversaries, weddings of nieces and nephews that Mom and Dad would have looked forward to are now accomplished without them. These holiday feasts and celebrations remain relevant to our family, and are richly celebrated, but are different in spirit as our family moves forward.

Did grief change our world? I would answer the question with a resounding YES! Slowly we were integrating the loss while at the same time reconstructing our family identity. The change did not so much involve the past as it did a decision to re-shape our future. Most of my siblings are now grandparents. Each family-set now creates their own particular rituals and ways of celebrating, sometimes modeled on what our parents did. Although family reunions, weddings, and special anniversaries continue to be celebrated with our entire large family, seasonal holidays are now celebrated with each family-set's own children and grandchildren, and maybe a few others. My siblings' families, whom I dearly love, and I, continue to find our way in this new world---a world where Mom and Dad's spirit is alive and well. However, the "hub" of the family which had been Mom and Dad's home and the major gathering place for family events is now gone.

ℬↃↄℛ

"The same stream of life that runs through my veins night and day runs through the world and dances in rhythmic measures. It is the same life that shoots in joy through the dust of the earth in numberless blades of grass and breaks into tumultuous waves of leaves and flowers."
-Rabindranath Tagore

ℬↃↄℛ

Hopefully, we are becoming better human beings because of our life-journeys with Mom and Dad. We all have a choice to find meaning in our lives because of what we have seen and heard, and the love we have received. Each of us siblings has shared our experience of transition into a new relationship with Mom and Dad. Several of my sibs have shared real-life incidences of speaking to Mom and Dad in heart and spirit. For example, some have felt up against a professional decision, or in need of prayers for one of their children or grandchildren, or want of assistance with a huge nerve-wracking project, or simply felt lost---only to find that Mom and Dad's spirit came through for them in a positive way they did not expect. Embracing Mom and Dad's death helps to calm the sting of their passing, and provides the gift of a brand new relationship of the heart.

ౠౚ

"In the depth of winter I finally learned that within me there lay an invisible summer."
Albert Camus

ౠౚ

Some people discover the positive qualities of loved ones after they are gone. Not so for us. We knew we were losing Mom and Dad as we had known them, and we knew them for a very long time. They had their flaws, but throughout life, their flaws seemed to pale in the brightness of their gifts. We know deeper joy because of their memory and spirit; and for their gift of love, we are exceedingly grateful to God.

REFLECTION:

For whom or what do you grieve?

What has helped you to grieve? What is or has not been helpful?

–15–

LEAVING A LEGACY

"In three words I can sum up
everything I've learned about life:
it goes on."

-Robert Frost

When parents die, we inherit a legacy. We also become the holder of traditions for future generations. I want to pay attention to Mom and Dad's strong legacy. I am often awed by the sacrifices they made so that their children could enjoy a quality of life, to be shared with all, regardless of race, color, or creed. They left us much. The feeling is that of a warm stream flowing through us from our parents' life values, and before them our grandparents' life values, and so on through generations. I have written some of this legacy in previous chapters, but I highlight three: faith, hope and love; "and the greatest of these is love."

Faith

"Your faith has made you whole", said Jesus. No one who knew my mother and father would doubt the fact that the depth and wholesomeness of their relationship with each other came from

ॐ

"Faith is the bird
that feels the light
and sings when the
dawn is still dark."
-Rabindranath Tagore

ॐ

103

their deep faith and trust. They were Christians in a non-conventional sense. Their practice of faith was less focused on the institutional church than it was on every day practices and lives of service. Their faith came through in so many little ways: for example, when guests entered their home they were welcomed with the following greeting said in the Czech language: "Praise be the Lord (bread-giver) Jesus Christ." Guests familiar with the prayer would respond: "Forever and ever, Amen."

After the "welcome" greeting, Dad would offer the guests a shot of his favorite Apricot Brandy, with Mom standing near. All would toast each other, and say: "Na zdravi", "to life!" The conversation would continue from there.

Praying as a family was a priority and a legacy from which we children have all benefited. Prayer before and after meals was consistently interwoven in the tapestry of our days, company present or not. Attending Sunday Eucharistic Liturgy as a family was never missed except for illness, the latter of which seemed rare in our family. During Advent and Lenten seasons, the rosary would be prayed as a family. Our traditional Christmas Eve dinner was akin to a seder meal, except that it was a meatless meal because Christ had not yet come. Dad led the prayers, some of which were spontaneous

ℬℭ

"I long to see you so that I may impart to you some spiritual gift to make you strong-that is, that you and I may be mutually encouraged by each other's faith."
-Romans 1:11-12

ℬℭ

and personal. Mom and Dad hosted this wonderful Christmas-Eve celebration throughout their lives, including the Christmas before their deaths in the summer of 2008.

Recognizing God in nature was another "faith" legacy. Trees, animals, stones, flowers, weeds were all symbols of God's story of strength, beauty, compassion and caring. In our growing up years, when we were hoeing in the garden, Dad would play word games with us and sometimes stop to explain the names of the weeds and offer a descriptive story. For example, he told us the story of the "redweed." The redweed is a green-leafed weed which carries the shape of a poinsettia blossom, except that it is green, shiny, and contains red, paint-brush-like streaks on each leaf. Dad said: "This is the weed that was growing through the stones at the foot of the cross where Jesus died. To this day it has red specks to remind us of how much Jesus loved us and how much he sacrificed for our sins." We did not question whether this was true or not as children; we believed it because Dad said it. He also told us the beautiful stories of other weeds like: queenanne's lace, mustard weed, and the ever present ragweed.

The reading and contemplation of Scripture was another powerful legacy. Mom and Dad kept a bible handy in the living room on the end table between their twin lazy-boy chairs. A simple word selected from Scripture could be the basis for a meditation. While taking care of Mom in her last weeks, Dad would quiet his mind and body in his easy chair, and allow the Word or

&⊃Ↄↄ

"I am the true vine."
-John 15:1

&⊃Ↄↄ

chosen Scripture passage to move through him like a gentle rain. Then he would sit for some time as if in a silent, loving presence with God. Was it a prayer of praise, gratitude, repentance, or intercession? We don't know. It all puts me in mind of the French Benedictine Monk, Dom Marmion, who under the inspiration of St. Benedict, put it this way:

We read	(lectio)
under the eye of God	(meditation)
until the heart is touched	(oratio)
and leaps to flame.	(contemplation)

In her book, <u>Welcome to the Wisdom of the World,</u> Benedictine Sister Joan Chittister beautifully describes this type of prayer.

When our loved ones die, they do not leave us. They remain. We cannot physically see them, but their spirit dances through our living. We need to pay attention to that dancing spirit, for it has much to say to us.

Hope

Elders like Mom and Dad who find freedom and creativity in their aging years and who share the wisdom accumulated over a life time, give everyone hope. For the most part, Mom and Dad viewed aging as a positive adventure. In their elder years, they discovered new sources of creativity in helping others whether through the St. Vincent de Paul society which works with the poor, or being part of other parish and civic activities, or spending time with grandchildren. They helped their grandchildren with homework; read to them; gave advice when asked; taught them to care about people, to sing, dance, and how to make things beautiful. At other times they simply enjoyed their grandchildren at their sides while baking, and/or engaging them in gardening activities.

St. Augustine wrote: "Hope has two lovely daughters, anger and courage, anger so that what should not be is not, and courage so that what should be is." I know without a doubt that our parents gave us hope---in doing justice, working for peace, living fully, and commitment in dying. Their spirit of hope also gave us courage to move forward. To the very end of their conscious dying,

ꙮꙮ

"Hope is the thing with feathers that perches in the soul and sings the tune without words and never stops at all."
-Emily Dickenson

ꙮꙮ

Mom and Dad's spirit of Hope seemed to lift the cloud of darkness from our hearts and perhaps kept us out of the shadow of despair.

Love

If there is any scripture passage that best depicts the life of Mom and Dad's relationship, it is the passage from 1 Corinthians 13: 4-13. "Love is always patient and kind; it is never jealous; love is never boastful or conceited; it is never rude or selfish; it does not take offense, and is not resentful. Love takes no pleasure in other people's sins but delights in the truth; it is always ready to excuse, to trust, to hope, and to endure whatever comes. Love does not come to an end."

ꙮꙮ

"Let loving lead your heart."
-Attar

ꙮꙮ

First and foremost, Mom and Dad loved their God. Then they loved each other: perhaps it was that they found God more deeply through their shared love and commitment to each other. The two were entwined into one, united in their love, faith, and sense of family. They carried a united front with us children, which instilled security and self-confidence. There was no splitting them, though we might have tried when there was a coveted desire at stake. I am sure they had their differences, and had to work things through. But I do not remember their arguing in front of us when we were children. The only thing I can figure is that when they had disagreements, they must have resolved them after we went to bed.

In my experience, compassion and listening on the part of Mom and Dad never seemed to be lost to self interest. It was comforting to know that Mom and Dad's love was consistently present. They knew they were far from perfect, yet they knew how to share love. No matter what our mistakes or faults, we could always count on their love, and for that matter, the love of the extended family. Mom and Dad had a strong sense of connection down through the generations. There was an ongoing continuity between the past, present, and future.

"Love recognizes no barriers. It jumps hurdles, leaps fences penetrates walls to arrive at its destination full of hope."
-Maya Angelou

Mom and Dad's affection threaded the energy of the family. We were all positively affected by their deep love for each other, for family, and for community. In their dying processes, Mom and Dad's fidelity to each unfolding moment continued to stitch the strength of goodness and integrity for all of us. This precious tapestry of love was interwoven with faith, hope, discipline, lightness and laughter. All went into the weave.

Love was also found in their advice-giving. In the most crucial decisions of my life, I would seek Mom and Dad's wisdom. One of the best pieces of long-standing advice I have ever received from anyone came from Dad. Many years ago when I was in the throes of making a decision whether to enter the convent, after almost being engaged to be married, I remember his words to me: *"...whatever helps you to love best, that you must do."* Dad's advice conveyed to me that whatever path I chose, if it was rooted in love, all would be well. I was young then, but that particular piece of advice continues to ground me as I approach my elder years.

Without a doubt, Mom and Dad's lives offered a feast from which many families can glean a rich daily meal.

REFLECTION:

What legacy do you wish to leave for family? For friends?

For the world community?

"It is possible I am pushing
through solid rock
as the ore lies alone.
I am such a long way in.
I can see no way through
and no space.
Everything is close to my face.
And everything close to my face
is stone.
I don't have much knowledge yet
in grief; so this darkness
makes me feel small.
You be the master.
Make yourself fierce.
Break in.
And then your great
transforming
Will happen to me.
And my great grief cry will
happen to you

-Rainer Marie Rilke

EPILOGUE

Mom and Dad left not a penny of debt. They had all bills, including their funerals paid for. Their gravesite and tombstone were chosen by them and in place several years before they passed to eternal life. It was important to them that they design their own tombstone. The simple, yet beautiful granite stone contains their names, wedding date, and dates of death etched on the front-face. Also carved into the front are the Czech Infant of Prague; and a dove etched over a simple cross, symbolizing the Holy Spirit and Peace. Carved into the back of the gravestone are all their children's names. Mom and Dad rest in peace together under beautiful trees, and near the major crucifix which stands at the center of Holy Trinity cemetery, where they had been parishioners throughout their sixty-seven years of marriage.

Both Mom and Dad died peacefully at home. Both treasured their family around them. Our family continues to learn from their simple yet heroic journeys.

****

Following are a few quotations from family members:

> "In my teenage years I was always thankful that Mom and Dad allowed me to do all the things I enjoyed; and never set a curfew when on a date or out with my friends. Dad always said: "you know the proper time to be in." If I was real late Mom and Dad never got mad, only asked what I did and did I have a good time. When I became a mother, I applied this wisdom to my own children, and it worked!"
>
> Daughter

*****

"Grandma had endless energy when it came to helping others, especially those in need. She was a life-time member of the St. Anthony Society where she donated endless hours of time, materials, and expertise in making Czech dolls, developing cookbooks, sewing and making products to sell for charity. She had high esteem for her heritage and helped to integrate her culture in everything she did.

Grandson

*****

"I've seen them share their home with a homeless person they didn't know because of their love for other people less fortunate."

Son-in-law

*****

"They brought God into their house, experienced and shared His love so that others could have the same feelings."

Daughter –in-law

*****

"When you would visit, whether by phone or in person, in their eyes, you were the most important person and you always felt loved and special."

Granddaughter

*****

"Our temptations for wrong were few because of their living example of goodness and faith. Even in our daily toil together, they showed us how to be happy and to make work light with conversation, word-games, and song."

Son

SERVICE AT THE GRAVESIDE

Dad had only one request for his funeral Liturgy: that his children sing the following song (in Czech) at his gravesite. The song reflects Dad's love for community, church, and country. However, the song's passion gets a bit lost in the translation.

Bože, Co's Ráčil

Bože, co's ráčil, před tisíci roky
Lord, what can I do for you? For a thousand years
Rozžati otcům světlo víry blahé.
the Father lighted our way with joyful faith.
:K tobě hlas prosby, z této vlasti vane.
We voice a request for you to cleanse our native country.
Dědictví otcův zachovej nám Pane:
Preserve our heritage to us Lord

Ochranu skytli v církvě svátem lune
Grant protection to the holy church
Učili národ znáti ctnosti krásu.
Teach the nation to understand virtuous beauty
:Od doby té nám světlo víry plane,
From time immemorial you illuminated the path of faith
Dědictví otcův zachovej nám Pane:
Preserve our heritage to us Lord

Získali láskou Kristu národ celý
Attain love of Christ in the whole nation
Život nám na vše věky zachovali.
and may we forever preserve your way of life

Fran A. Repka

**:Nezhyne rod, jenž věřit neustane
Dědictví otcův zachovej nám Pane:**
Preserve our heritage to us Lord.

ACKNOWLEDGEMENTS

Until recently, I had no intention of writing "Dying with Grace." What was intended as an article, turned out to be a small book. Few people knew I was writing it. Nevertheless, I would like to acknowledge two of my wisdom-friends, Mary Ann Fuerst, RSM and Annette Boyle, IHM, who encouraged me to put the experience of Dad's capacity to die with such dignity and grace into words. Mary Ann knew my father, Annette did not. Several other friends encouraged me along the way.

Our writing group: Ann Baumgardner, Marie Nicholson, and Robin O'Neal-Kissel kept me writing when I felt like giving up because I was too overwhelmed with other full-time commitments. They also offered helpful suggestions. In addition, Ann went the extra mile to patiently walk me through computer challenges. I owe each of them a debt of gratitude.

A special thanks goes to Mary Perpetua Overbeck, RSM for painstakingly reviewing this manuscript for grammatical and spelling errors. I also thank my Sisters in Mercy who supported me before, during, and after my parents' passing.

Last, but certainly not least, I thank all those who knew my parents, and deeply loved them, particularly members of my family, several of whom contributed to the content of this book, and all of whom are part of the weave of the colorful fabric we call "the Repka Clan."

I will never be satisfied with what I have written; for every time I re-read a portion of this book, I see something I could have done differently. It is what it is.

REFERENCES

1. James Martin, S.J., *The Jesuit Guide to (Almost) Everything.* New York, New York: HarperCollins Publishers, 2010, p. 144. Quotation in text used with permission from publisher.

2. Jim Forest, *The Road to Emmaus: Pilgrimage as a Way of Life.* New York: Orbis Books, 2007, p. 109. Quotation in text used with permission from publisher.

3. Miriam Therese Winter, MM, Source: *WomanWisdom: A Feminist Lectionary and Psalter; Women of the Hebrew Scriptures: Part One.* New York: Crossroad Publishing Co. Poem used with permission from Miriam Therese Winter, Medical Mission Sisters.

4. Joan Chittister, OSB, *Illuminated Life: Monastic Wisdom for Seekers of Light:. Maryknoll.* NY Orbis Books, 2000, p. 81. Quotation in text used with permission from publisher.

Other References

Joan Chittister, OSB, *Welcome to the Wisdom of the World.* Grand Rapids, Michigan: Wm B. Eerdmans Publishing Co., 2007.

Daniel Ladinsky, *Love Poems from God.* Viking Penguin, a division of Penguin Group (USA), Inc, 2002.

Pierre Teilhard de Chardin, *Hymn of the Universe.* New York, New York: Harper & Row, Inc, 1965.

Rabindranath Tagore, *Selected Poems*. Translated by William Radice. London: Penguin Books, 1994.

Brian Swimme, *The Hidden Heart of the Cosmos*. Maryknoll, New York: Orbis Books, 1996.

Eckhart Tolle, *The Power of Now*. Novato, CA: .New World Library, 2004, p190.

Miriam Therese Winter, *WomanWord*. New York, NY: The Crossword Publishing Company, 1990.

Scripture quotes edited and adapted from:

Mercy Prayer Book: Institute of the Sisters of Mercy of the Americas, 1998.

The New Revised Standard Version Bible, copyright 1989 by the Division of Christian Education of the National Council of the Churches of Christ in the USA.

APPENDIX I

CHRISTMAS EVE TRADITION

It was the custom in our family to fast on Christmas Eve day until sundown. This was honored for most of my adult years (though when we were small children we were given mini snacks). It was thought that if one fasted until Christmas Eve dinner (at evening), one would see the golden pig. The meaning of the golden pig was vague, but we knew it had something to do with prosperity and health for the coming year. We also knew that fasting was considered important as we waited for Jesus to come. I will attempt to share the "phases" of this special Repka-family Christmas celebration.

Everyone arrived at Mom and Dad's home by noon on Christmas Eve. Mom and Dad greeted each family separately. Before each family entered, they stood at the doorway and said the following Christmas Greeting prayer in Czech:

Vínsujem vám štastné
A veselé svátký
Krista Pána narozeniny
Na statečku rozmnožení
Co jsme si od Pána Boha vižadali
Předně zdravy pokoj svatý
A posmrti nebeské královstvi
Pochválen bud´ Pán Ježiš Kristus!

Roughly translated:
We wish you
a happy and merry holiday
on the birthday of Christ the Lord.
What we wish you
from our Lord God:
Blessings of health, peace, and
a holy room in the heavenly Kingdom after death.
The Lord God Jesus Christ bless you.

Mom and Dad then responded with:
A věky vekův. Amen
For ever and ever. Amen

An hour or so after everyone had arrived, Santa Claus came from afar with his sleigh full of toys. Santa had an interesting route. He would come through the snow-covered forty-acre woods surrounding my parents home, jingling his bells while at the same time offering a merry ho-ho-ho, loud enough for the children to hear. Holding infants and small children in our arms, we would first observe Santa through the large picture windows, hoping to assuage any fear the children might experience when Santa entered our parent's home. Most of the children were as excited as they could be; periodically there would be a niece or nephew who was at least temporarily fearful. While distributing the gifts, every adult and child had an opportunity to sit on Santa's lap. Santa would have something special to say to each one, for Santa was played by an uncle, older brother, or a neighbor, all of whom knew the family.

The rest of the afternoon was spent talking, sharing, and exchanging excitement over who had whose name for their Secret Santa. Around 5:30 pm the family proceeded to the downstairs large living room where all was in readiness for the traditional Czech Christmas Eve dinner.

The Christmas Eve traditional meal is a sit-down meal with family members and a couple of guests present. My mother was an artist and spent weeks decorating and preparing the variety of foods to be consumed at this special meal, -----unlike any other kind of dinner we have all year. The tables were beautifully prepared with white linen table cloths, linen napkins, candles, and decorative centerpieces. Stacks of my parents' finest china and crystal goblets adorned each place-setting (Dad would never tolerate paper plates or plastic ware). Walls and windows were decorated with Christmas finery: golden bells, red velvet ribbon, Christmas lights, Christmas bulbs, garland, and a Christmas tree both upstairs and downstairs. The setting was a vision of beauty in itself. It was customary to invite a guest who had no one else with whom to celebrate Christmas, and sometimes the parish priest attended as well.

The meal began with everyone standing at their places and Dad leading the prayers. Prayers were said in Czech (several Our Father's and Hail Mary's) and spontaneous prayers in English. We prayed prayers of gratitude for all God's favors and blessings on the family in the past year. We prayed, by name, for all those who died in current and past years. We prayed for anyone in the family who was ill, had losses or hardships of any kind. We prayed for world peace and for world leaders. We prayed for good health, good jobs and blessings in the future. The little ones in high-chairs would sometimes be asleep by the end of the prayers. As small children I remember we would sometimes burst into giggling fits during the many prayers. Grandfather Repka led the prayers when we were children. When Grandfather died, Dad began to lead the prayers. Our nuclear family had grown by leaps and bounds.

As adults we treasured this Christmas ritual, and hung on to every spoken word. Dad's spontaneous prayers were special and very meaningful. He was a poetic man of great depth, and spoke in profound ways. Mom lovingly stood by his side, reminding him of anything he might forget in leading the prayers. Always, Dad would give gratitude to God for Mom first and foremost. When he spoke of his children, he called us his "jewels"; and would share his hopes and dreams for our family. Then we prayed for the community and our world. In the last two Christmases prior to his passing, Dad had to stop often, as tears of gratitude would well up in him. Of course the rest of us would then tear up as well.

To continue with the meal: first comes the oplatky, i.e., unleavened bread, obtained through the Catholic Archdiocese with special permission. This part of the ritual is a reminder of God's chosen people eating unleavened bread on their way to the Promised Land. For Christians it is a reminder that Christ is coming, but not here yet. Each adult and child is given a large piece of unleavened bread (wafer-like), by my parents. Mom would hand the oplatky one by one to Dad, who in turn sprinkled each wafer with home-made honey (Dad was a beekeeper on the side), and passed the wafer to each person present. This took awhile. This ritual is followed by everyone receiving a small goblet of hot tody (mixture of straight whiskey, butter, and honey). Children drank hot cider. Again, Dad poured each one separately, blessed it, and passed a goblet to each one present. It was after drinking the hot, rather potent tody, that people talked with humor about seeing or not-seeing the "golden-pig."

The unleavened bread and hot tody rituals were followed by a meatless mushroom soup with dumplings, called "kiselice." Kiselice is a delicious wild-mushroom cream soup served with dumplings and seasoned specifically for this Christmas Eve Celebration. According to an old Czech myth, wild mushrooms (as well as honey and garlic) are believed to have special powers of strengthening and protecting the self, and are often ascribed a heavenly origin. For Dad, garlic cured everything that ailed you, and was the best preventative. For those of us with Czech heritage, kiselice was most enjoyable, and many of our in-laws who were not Czech in heritage found it savory as well. The few who did not care for kiselice were provided an alternative of rice soup with mini egg-drop noodles. The meatless soups are symbolic of the simplicity of waiting for Jesus in Hope and quenching the day's fast.

After the soup phase of the meal, we partook of a little cream-of-wheat to celebrate the first fruits of the spring harvest, and beans-and-barley to celebrate the first fruits of the fall harvest. Again these are special recipes specific for this Christmas feast. The main course consists of fish. Our generation tends to serve fresh jumbo shrimp, and a specially prepared tuna dish. In my grandmother's and grandfather's time, fresh-water fish, tuna, and herring were served. This phase of the meal is accompanied by lime-jello salad and a prune dish.

At the end of the meal, a variety of Czech homemade desserts are enjoyed, along with fresh fruit and nuts; buchty, boleske, pupaki, rohlicky, apricot stars, apricot crescents, smetanove trubecki, makova nadivka, orechova nadivka, makova zavin, cottage-cheese-filled pastries, apple strudle, and so on, to name a few of the desserts. Conversation flows freely and non-stop. By this time it is pitch dark outdoors, but light and lively indoors.

After this special Czech Christmas Eve meal, we gathered in the upper living room of my parents' home where earlier in the day we had exchanged Christmas presents. All remained aglow with Christmas tree lights and decorations. Mom's artistic touch was everywhere. When all were settled we commenced singing every Christmas Carol in the universe, and I mean every Christmas carol anyone can think of, including the 12 days of Christmas with little sub-groups doing each part. We never needed song books for we sang the songs so often that even the children knew many of the lyrics by heart. It was tradition to end this song-fest with "Silent Night"----singing all three verses---and at the very end, gently *humming* an extra verse. It was at this point that we shut off all the lamps, leaving only the Christmas tree lights aglow, and a few candles which were interspersed throughout the living room.

After the song-fest, Dad and Mom would share words of gratitude for their children, grand-children, and great-grandchildren. On Mom and Dad's last Christmas, (of course no one knowing it would be their last), Dad said: "If heaven is anything like this, I am ready" and "….heaven couldn't be better than this moment." How prophetic were his words! As Christmas Eve ended, those who wished attended Midnight Mass to celebrate Jesus' having been born.

This is my recollection. I wish I could adequately convey the warmth, closeness, joy, and love I consistently experienced on this special family day. The Christmas prior to their summer deaths, Mom and Dad led the celebration. Now they are gone. Our Christmas Eve tradition continues in some of my siblings' families' homes. Always and forever, Mom and Dad are present in spirit.

PRAYERS: CHRISTMAS EVE TRADITION

Známeni sv. Kríže
THE SIGN OF THE CROSS

Ve jmenu Otce, i Syna, i Ducha Svatého. Amen

O Modlitbe Pane
THE LORD'S PRAYER

Otče náš, Jenž jsi na nebesích, posvěť se jméno Tvé
Our father, Who art in heaven, hallowed be Thy name

Přijd království Tvé, buď vůle Tvá, jako v nebi tak I na zemi
Thy kingdom come, thy will be done, on earth as it is in heaven

Chléb naš vezdejši dejž nám dnes
Give us this day our daily bread

A odpusť nám naše viny, jakož I my od pouštíme našim vinníkům
And forgive us our trespasses, as we forgive those who trespass against us

A neuvoď nas v pokušení, ale zbav nás od zlého. Amen
And lead us not into temptation, but deliver us from evil. Amen

Zdrávas Maria
THE HAIL MARY

Zdrávas Maria, milosti plná! Pán s tebou
Hail Mary, full of grace! The Lord is with thee

Požehnaná tys mezi ženami, a požehnaný plod života tvého, Ježiš
Blessed art thou among women, and blessed is the fruit of thy womb, Jesus

Svatá Maria, Matko Boží, pros za nás hříšné
Holy Mary, Mother of God, pray for us sinners

nyní i v hodinu smrti naší. Amen
now and at the hour of our death. Amen

Sláva
GLORY BE

Sláva Otci i Synu i Duchu Svatému
Glory be to the Father and to the Son and to the Holy Spirit

Jakož byla na počátku, nýni, i vyždycký, na věky vekův. Amen
As is was in the beginning, is now, and ever shall be, world without end. Amen

APPENDIX II
RHYTHM AND RITUAL

The following activities slowly came into place and appeared to contribute to a peaceful atmosphere for Dad:

- Before Dad arrived home, we created a pleasant environment conducive to comfort, quiet, and hospitality. Dad's hospice bed was placed near a very large picture window where he could view nature which was important to him. In this setting he could rest, see the trees, hear the birds, and visit family and other guests--- all in a room familiar to him.

- Including Dad in any decision-making helped maintain his dignity. He wanted others to talk *with* him, not about him. Given the fact that Dad had lost complete control of his body, inclusion in decision-making became particularly salient.

- We established a comfortable routine of good physical care, comfort, intimacy, sleep and rest from day one. In the morning: a bath, a visit from the hospice nurse to clean and pack his open wound, prayer, and listening to the news. In the afternoon and evening it varied. Sometimes the afternoon was reserved for unfinished business and/or visiting relatives, friends, and neighbors. Each night, a family member slept near Dad's hospice bed. Having someone near, but not intrusive, was calming for him.

- Open-ended "time" with loved ones was essential. Dad was clear about not wanting to place time limits on whatever he chose to do.

- Prayer (private and public) specifically meaningful to Dad was of essence. See Chapter on the "Power of Prayer."

- Providing a rhythm of silence and engagement/visiting was important for Dad's psychic health. Dad was an introvert by nature and although he enjoyed company, he also needed his naps and time for silence.

- Supporting communication that was timely, honest, and open with family, friends and caregivers. Open communication also provided an opportunity for Dad to discuss his pending death if he desired.

- Providing the time as well as legal and financial assistance for finalizing financial documents and other unfinished business requested by Dad. We also met Dad's request to discuss funeral arrangements.

- Always empathy, not sympathy. Accurate empathy seemed to help Dad relax. Sympathy was irritating to him. Empathy was especially helpful when Dad was grieving Mom's very recent death. Empathy and time to grieve other losses was also essential.

APPENDIX III

Poem written two months after Helen and Frank's passing,-- as part of the grieving process.

THEY ARE GONE

They are gone, our dear parents...
Though I cannot *SEE* them,
    their reflections in nature
      are ubiquitous...
in colorful autumn trees
in leaves gently falling
in the calm, serene lake
in the blue, sun-lit sky
in a warm, comforting breeze
in frolicking birds and ducks
in the coordination of flying geese
in the graceful, leaping deer
in the cool night air.

I *HEAR* them
when nature calls out their names...
in birds warbling and singing
squirrels gathering nuts for winter's survival
fish jumping with delight
geese "honking"
ducks quacking
dogs barking.

children playing
people laughing
music playing
family singing.

Though I cannot TOUCH them
Mom and Dad seem to be everywhere...
when I awake in the morning
when I pray
when I make an omelet
when I delight in beauty all around me
when I sit on the porch in quiet
when I care about things
when I read
when I enjoy being with people
when I love others
when I weep
when I dance
when I share in Eucharist.

They are here, but not here.
A surreal awakening;
I cannot bring them back
    as they were before,
Yet I know they are with me,
    embracing me
ever new, ever holy.

Fran A. Repka, rsm

CPSIA information can be obtained at www.ICGtesting.com
Printed in the USA
BVOW011120110112

280239BV00003B/2/P